Learning the Ropes

Other books by Bill Ransom

Finding True North, Copper Canyon Press
Waving Arms at the Blind, Copper Canyon Press
The Single Man Looks at Winter, Empty Bowl Press
Last Call, Blue Begonia Press
Last Rites, Brooding Heron Press
The Jesus Incident (with Frank Herbert), Putnam/Berkley
The Lazarus Effect (with Frank Herbert), Putnam/Berkley
The Ascension Factor (with Frank Herbert), Putnam/Ace
Jaguar, Ace
Semaphore, Tangram Press
ViraVax, Ace
Burn, Ace

Bill Ransom

Learning the Ropes

*A Creative
Autobiography*

UTAH STATE UNIVERSITY PRESS
Logan, Utah

Utah State University Press
Logan, Utah 84322–7800

Introduction copyright © 1995 by Jim Heynen.
Cover painting: "Curved Space-Time" by Susan Fleming. Used by permission.
Cover design: Barbara Yale-Read
Typography by WolfPack

Library of Congress Cataloging-in-Publication Data

Ransom, Bill.
    Learning the ropes : a creative autobiography / Bill Ransom.
      p. cm.
    ISBN 0–87421–190–5
    1. Ransom, Bill—Biography.   2. Authors, American—20th century—Biography.
I. Title.
    PS3568.A577Z468 1995
    813'.54—dc20
      [B]   95–4342
                                                                          CIP

For my daughter, Hali Kalae Johnson, with love.

Acknowledgments

THANKS to those people who made this book possible: Editors Susan Allison, The Berkley Publishing Group, Jim Bodeen, Blue Begonia Press, Sam and Sally Green, Brooding Heron Press, Sam Hamill, Copper Canyon Press, Jerry Reddan, Tangram Press, Michael Spooner, Utah State University Press; friends Ken Brewer, Dave Hart, Jim Heynen, Sally Kranzler, Ron Lampard, David Lee, Dick and Johanna Marquis, Pierr Morgan, Gary Robertson; the *Kamui* captain and crew, the ER team at Jefferson General Hospital, the firefighters at Jefferson County Fire District #6 and Port Townsend Fire Department, "The FogFarm"; mis compañeros de centroamerica Beatriz, Cristina, y Adriana Alcaine, Roberto Cañas, Carolyn Forché, Margarita Herrera, Steve Kimball, Roger Lutz, Jeff MacKinnon, Guillermo Martínez, Sister Siena Schmitt, Ron Womach; agents Ralph Vicinanza and Chris Lotts.

Contents

Introduction

Jim Heynen

Words put you here, not stars. . . .
Words, not God. Words.
Bill Ransom, *Instruction at the Gate*

BILL Ransom's *Learning the Ropes* is to autobiographies what *Gulliver's Travels* is to travel manuals. The genre cannot hold it. I think of contemporary writers like Kathleen Norris whose *Dakota* is more than another book about place: it is a "spiritual geography." I am reminded, too, of writers like Lewis Thomas and Oliver Sacks, who alter reader expectations in what have conventionally been fact- and theory-laden disciplines. In this innovative collage, Ransom is among the writers who forge into new territory, who twist our expectation and "make it new." Rather than confronting an autobiographer's purported exact recollections, we know in reading Ransom's book that what might have been real has been infused with the transforming power of the imagination. And this is true both in the individual selections and in the collage effect of several forms leaning together: poems, short stories, essays, and excerpts from novels. I find this book on the cutting edge of genre-making.

Together, the selections that make up the book are not only a compelling sampling of works from a prolific writer at midlife, they constitute what the book promises to be: a creative autobiography. As "autobiography" it suggests a life worth reflecting upon; as "creative" it demonstrates the rewards of the collage-effect rendered through the varied lenses of different genres. It's as if the same story material were given to different movie producers: the central themes may be similar, but the presentations are not.

If the opening poem tells us that Ransom puts his hope in words, not stars, then we must notice how quickly the words turn to flesh in such sensuously rich poems as "A Beginning" in which he writes

if berries tell the story
let them sing from the bushes
and blend their thin red voices
into a chorus of flesh.

But the book also suggests that if we must live in the flesh, we must also go beyond what we know through the senses into the realm of values and moral questions. For my money, no writer worth his or her salt makes these moral questions simplistic. Imaginative writers worth reading are always of two minds—like Toni Morrison, always embracing the ambiguity of good and evil. And Ransom does not look for the easy answers through the stories of his characters. Notice, for example, how the good Catholic boys who are not in form school behave in the first story of the collection, "Hammering Jesus." The story does not hesitate to embrace the lives of ignorant and innocent youth while also showing the cruelty implicit to it. And like other significant moral writers of our time, Ransom does not excuse his players. The human condition may be tough, he seems to say, but we are still responsible for what happens to us. It's as if we are the makers of our own undoing. As he writes in the poem "Food Chain," "We are the only netted fish who pull our own nets."

I have known Bill Ransom for over twenty years. I knew him first as a poet active in the Artists in Schools programs that flourished around the country in the 1970's, then as an innovative arts administrator who founded the well-known writing program through Centrum Foundation at Fort Worden in Port Townsend, Washington. I knew him as the parent of the daughter he celebrates and remembers in many of his poems. I knew him as an athlete long after he distinguished himself in high school and college athletics. The Ransom of some years later was someone who could still run a marathon and someone who still carried in his hands the tactile memories of his boxing father. And I have known him as someone who has not forgotten the discipline of the manual labor he knew so well as a teenager in the area around Puyallup. He can build a house; he can dig a ditch. I have known him as he ventured off into the discipline of science fiction writing, co-authoring three novels with Frank Herbert. I watched his vision of the world expand in his concerns for Central America and the possibility of terrorism in all of our futures. In the Ransom autobiography that has not reached these pages explicitly, I have known a person who gives teeth to his vision, who makes concrete what is abstract, who localizes what is general. When he became concerned about Central America, he prepared to visit there by learning Spanish. When he became concerned about the physical welfare of others both locally and abroad, he became a certified Emergency Medical Technician. For reasons that are greater than those hinted at in one of the stories in this collection, he became a trained firefighter. In short, the Ransom who is not explicitly on the page is a kind of compassionate survivalist. Some people might be described as optimists who do nothing to warrant optimism. I would describe the off-the-page Ransom as a pessimist who does everything he can to keep his worst fears from coming true.

If we might say, "as one lives, so one writes," we might conclude that the life and writing of Bill Ransom are clearly the products of a sensibility inclined toward personal, familial, community and world survival. Some of the writing may be confessional, but never in a solipsistic way. We may guess correctly that the man writing has indeed spent many work hours among the berry harvesters near his hometown of Puyallup, that he did indeed have a troublesome father who was a professional boxer, that he did work in an airplane plant during the Vietnam War, that he was an EMT and that he has been a volunteer fireman, that he was educated in religion, that he does have a daughter who is dear to him, that he has spent working time in troubled Central America, and that he has earned an appreciation for the flora of the Pacific Northwest.

Ransom's creative autobiography covers the range from the uplifting, visionary "Last Rites" with its glyph series, to the dark humor of a poem like "Living Will," which begins "Burn me./ Pay the fine. . . ." But what Ransom's autobiography shows most of all is that the life of this writer's imagination parallels the life he lives among humankind: and it is a life as a quest. The quest is for knowledge, for understanding

of man's inhumanity to man, and for transcendence beyond the insistent limitations of human possibility.

If you are inclined to approach this book as a literary critic, you will
find a disciplined writer who has operated exceptionally well in several
forms. I suspect you will find, as have I, that some of his short stories
can take their place among the best of Raymond Carver's: the same
kind of people working with inadequate resources to make sense of
their lives. As with Carver, we hear authorial compassion for the characters, but with little hope for their well-being in a cruel world. The
poems and excerpts also tend to move toward the hard truths of the
world. The entire book is a kind of David and Goliath story: the small
fist of hope and love against ubiquitous—personal, cultural, and global—forces of destruction and despair.

The journey that this book takes is not for the faint of heart. Indeed,
it is often dark, and the voice of the artist behind the work sometimes
seems that of the pessimist or the lonely outsider. But if Ransom's
vision persistently strays from the optimistic, one might well remember
the words of the Northwest poet Theodore Roethke: "What's madness
but nobility of soul/ At odds with circumstance?" Indeed, Ransom's
work is ruthlessly sane—the painful sanity of showing what is and
might be—and ruthlessly at odds with much of the circumstance of his
time. The final essays and stories from Central America and the excerpt
from his novel ViraVax are a kind of call to alarm. As Ransom sees it,
the cruelty that ran rampant there could easily be a prelude to what
might happen here.

I challenge you as a reader to question yourself as you encounter the
stories and images collected here from another person's real and imaginative life. As you finish each poem, each story, each essay, I predict
you will be drawn steadily into self-examination—of our shared global
culture and of your more immediate community and personal culture.
I believe you will find that Ransom's quest for physical and spiritual
survival is your own as well.

1

Instruction at the Gate

At the gateway to the beast
your arms brim with dead leaves.
Words, not fate, put you here.

Sweet breath of the beast wets this fall air.
That wrist of sunlight snagged in the weeds

feel the pulse, yes
the beast feels it, too.

Bury your face in the leaves, breathe
prepare to teach the beast: *these.*

Words put you here, not stars.

Listen to its supple flex across the weeds,
that cupped palm of sunlight.
Words, not God. Words.

A Beginning

Bones should never tell a story to a bad beginner.
James Welch

Then let it be flesh
or the firm crush of strawberries
staining a basket.

Let it be fresh as the story itself:
hands brushing nipples,
the tumble of the first berry
into a tight clean basket.

But if berries tell the story,
let them sing from the bushes
and blend their thin red voices
into a chorus of flesh
and baskets left empty in the grass.

Reunión

para Carolina

Our hands forget the names of the dead
make promises we call love
unbutton, unhook, unzip winter.

This moan is the season
our tongues are tied to.

The afternoon drowses beside a gray stone.
Your scent, a lapful of petals
our bodies a flutter of uncooped birds.

The Lost

Autumn whistles wind home between rocks
and bends the one bunch of grasses down.

A pair of nighthawks strains at their wings
outfluttering the few fat moths.

We bed down here in this gully
to finger the stops in our thin flute of night.

Hammering Jesus

I PULLED three really nice nails out of a board at the dump. I don't remember where I got the hammer, but I used it to tap the nails straight on the sidewalk. The big ones like the three I got to nail Jesus don't straighten very easy. Sometimes you pinch your finger. You put the hump side up and hit it, and the hammer bounces right up in the air. A hammer works a lot better than a rock.

Sometimes we tear off some caps from a roll and hit them with a hammer on the sidewalk. When they pop, they bounce your hammer a little bit. One day I hammered a whole roll of caps at once and popped some powder into my eye. It really hurt. I had to wear a bandage on both eyes and I couldn't go to school all week.

I got in trouble because I wasn't supposed to have the hammer any-more after I nailed my sister into the chicken wire. All she wants to do is sit and play in the dirt, anyway, and I had that chicken wire that me and Big Tim found at the dump. I put her toys in the corner where Robbie Dobson's house meets our house, then nailed up the chicken wire. She stayed in there okay but Mom got mad when she came home from work.

My sister broke her arm in the swing, so she couldn't come out and play Jesus with us. She hit me with her cast and it really hurt. But not as bad as that powder.

The policeman told me they don't have radios in form school. I like the radio. I'm in Catholic school now. I'm in second grade and I can already read a book. I get to read any time I want to in the coat room.

Robbie Dobson doesn't go to Catholic school. I don't know, maybe he goes to form school. He takes the 38th street bus, I take the Mani-tou. I forgot to get off at school one day and rode all the way to Mani-tou. When I tried to walk back, I got lost in the cemetery, and the lawn mower man called the police. Dad had to come get me and he really hates riding on the bus. He gets in fights. He got in a fight on the way home with a man who looked at him.

There was me, Janet Sue, Little Tim and Big Tim, and Robbie to play Jesus.

"You all know who Jesus is?" I asked.

Everybody knew.

"Well, who wants to be Jesus?"

Robbie Dobson and Janet Sue both said, "I do, I do."

"You can't be Jesus, you're a girl," Robbie said.

Big Tim and Little Tim just waited to see who they could be, they didn't want to be Jesus.

So Robbie Dobson got to be Jesus, and Janet Sue was Mary and Little Tim carried the can with the nails. Me and Big Tim were the soldiers.

We went behind where Big Tim's house and Little Tim's house come together. I had Robbie Dobson back up against Little Tim's wall and stretch out his arms.

"Will it hurt?"

I told him it wouldn't hurt, and showed him my hand.

"See? You go in this soft part between the bones. It just pinches a little bit, that's all."

He said if it hurt I'd better stop, and I did. I think I hammered a bone. But then I couldn't get the nail out and he was stuck to Little Tim's wall. He was crying and I tried to get the nail out but the hammer kept smashing his fingers and he kept hitting me with his other hand.

Sister Nathalie told me that Jesus never hit.

Little Tim's mom came running and got the nail out. She was really mad. She called Robbie Dobson's mom. She called the police, and they called my dad. He's catching the bus home from the gym. He hates riding the bus, and he's really going to be mad.

I don't know what everybody's so *mad* about. I would have let Robbie Dobson nail *me* up, but *he* was the one who wanted to be Jesus.

Uncle Hungry

The boy Rafferty dragged stones to the uncle's grave to prop up the lid of an old toolbox that he'd inscribed with "Uncle Hungry" in neat, black letters. Above and below the name, and to either side of it, four clusters of wings caught the rising March sun and licked the bleached backdrop of wood like cold flame. Rafferty dropped the young sack of his body down on the gravetop and watched a finger of sun try to pry apart the iron lips of the sky.

The wind that whipped around the corner of the barn was the last of the night wind running for cover. The boy was tired, sweaty from the night's digging. The wind that had teeth in it last night passed him this morning without a snap. Along this side of the barn, the morning-sun side, a scatter of crocuses nodded their lavender heads. The uncle saved those bulbs an extra year before planting, just to be safe.

"Quiet as a grave," the older man might have said. Rafferty said it for him and added the quick snort that his uncle used for a laugh. Wind-sighs, the raspy rattle of loose dust off the stone-tops, his crow on the barn roof stretching its right wing out—it was as though everything was waiting for Uncle to show up so they could get on with things.

Right after the hatch, inside the still, things were much more quiet than this. Those quiet days dragged into months, a year, two years thick with fear, with knives in the night and the heavy stink of rotting flesh from the barn and from the spring. Rafferty fingered one of the bronze flutterings tacked to the box lid—a clump of brittle, translucent wings. Inside the barn, bushels of these wings filled bins along one wall. His uncle, or the man he called uncle, saved them from those first terrifying months of the hatch.

Nothing like it since, the boy thought.

The voice in his mind was older than he remembered. Those bright buzzing things crawled out of the ground that day and they took wing after a spring shower. He remembered seeing the sun during the shower, and a rainbow.

Five years back, Rafferty was five years old. He was playing with his cousin and sitting on a sidewalk when the shower caught them and they heard the first dry rattling of wings rise around them with the heavy wet spatter of the drops.

None of the things attacked them, but when they flew they rasped out an unpleasant scrape against the air and when they landed on him their stiff, stiltlike legs scratched his neck and hands. The neighbor lady screamed, and other screams opened up all down the street. The neighbor scooped him and his cousin up into the heavy folds of her body and grunted them into her house. Over her shoulder, as the screen door slammed, the thousands of bronze wings caught the glint of the after-shower sun.

Hundreds of the things pushed up out of gardens and gravel driveways; from lawns like the neighbor's and from hillsides they unfolded their dazzling wings and joined the bronze cloud rolling across the countryside. It was like watching fire disassemble a log. While the neighbor woman babbled into the telephone, Rafferty and his cousin knelt at the living-room window and listened to the scrabble of hard little bodies against the walls outside.

The things had bodies bigger than a man's finger. They were orange with yellow bellies and their finely veined translucent wings stretched almost a foot from tip to tip. Each one of the things had four wings and six bristly legs, but it was difficult to think of them one at a time when the walls, the lawns and streets, the air itself was already filled with them and with the dry rattle of the wings. The window was acrawl with them and he remembered being fascinated with the bob and pulse of the thousands of yellow bellies against the glass.

The neighbor woman yanked him away from the window and pulled the shades. When she finally took him out of the house he was rolled in a blanket so that he couldn't see or hear anything. He felt the car swerve and lurch, stop and back up, turn. This happened several times and all the while he felt the blanketed silent body of his cousin bounce the seat beside him.

Then the car lurched once and tipped, tipped and kept going over. Rafferty was jolted and slammed all over the back seat and when the rolling stopped he was afraid to look out of the blanket. He was pinned so tight his chest and back felt like they met each other, and he only had the freedom to move one arm and his head. He worked the blanket from across his face and discovered that he was lying on the ceiling of the car with his head lower than the rest of him.

The back seat had popped loose to wedge him in. He couldn't see any sign of his cousin. The neighbor woman was just a series of gurgles and gasps on the other side of the seat. The noises came farther and farther apart and finally stopped. The roof of the car underneath him was covered with shards of broken glass, cigarette butts and hair curlers.

Rafferty could hardly breathe with the seat jamming him in so tight. He tried to shove it away but it wouldn't budge. He panted tiny, burning breaths from the effort, and a lot of small black spots in front of his eyes melted into one big one. He wasn't really asleep, he hadn't caught his breath yet, but he knew he wasn't getting out of there.

As soon as he knew he couldn't get out, he had to go to the bathroom. He beat on the back of the seat, but that made the spots come back so he started crying, but that hurt, too. Outside, the familiar rasp and tick of those bright bugs played against the metal of the car, and by the time Rafferty had wet himself the inside of the car was crawling with them. They didn't bite or sting, they just crawled over him with their stickery feet.

He was wedged inside there with them for four days before he ate the first one. It wouldn't get out of his face even when he batted it away. He caught it by the root of its wings with his free hand, shook it once and popped it into his mouth. His lips were cracked and his tongue thick with thirst.

What happened between Rafferty and the bug was purely some kind of reflex. He kept hold of the wings and spit out the legs because they were long and skinny and they stuck in his throat. He lost count of the days and thought of the rest of the bugs that he ate as corn dogs. A scattering of wings and legs littered the roof under his head, little bronze-petaled flowers with dark brown stalks. He disregarded the incredible stench that rolled in from the front seat.

He learned to sleep with the scuttle of things across his face, learned that crying only made his throat sore, learned that sometimes there was no border between waking and dreams.

Out of a dream of drinking from the faucet behind his grandparents' house he heard the heavy crunch of footsteps and a clatter of gravel against the side of the car.

"Verna!" a hoarse voice shouted, a male voice. "Verna?"

Someone pulled the glass out of the side window in front.

"Oh, no," the voice whispered, then coughed. "Verna."

Someone sat down outside the car and slumped against it. Rafferty heard him gasping and gagging out there. He listened to everything as though he perched on a tree limb above the whole broken scene. He knew this: If he didn't speak, the man's voice outside would leave and he would die there. He knew this without knowing much about death, without seeing death except for the brittle creatures that he snatched from the seat-back and stuffed into his mouth. What his senses told him about what was happening to the neighbor woman in the front seat unlocked his silence.

"Hungry," his throat managed to hiss out. The word sounded like the struggle of dry wings against steel.

"Hungry."

Until the strong hands of the blue-eyed man unrolled him from the blanket and laid him on the slope outside the car, Rafferty had no idea how bad he smelled. The area around him was not the seething mass of bugs that it had been a few days before, but there were still plenty of them around. The air outside the car made him feel clean again and the places that had stopped hurting in the car started to throb now that he was free. Even though the breeze had a chill to it, he lay still and bathed in the luxury of clean air. He sucked at the water-bottle that the stranger offered him and lay still.

Verna's brother felt his head, his back, his arms and legs. Rafferty moved his fingers and toes when asked and noticed, behind the thin man who prodded and pulled at him, that nowhere did he see any grass, any of the new spring leaves. Around them, as far as he could see from the hillside, the leafless and barkless trees shone pale in the afternoon's glare.

Rafferty woke up in bed between smooth, clean sheets, to cramps in the stomach and visions of those bright bronze bugs just out of reach. He smelled coffee and fried bacon, and he felt the itch of bandages taped to his chest, his back and shoulder. The bandage between his shoulder-blades itched the most.

"Stop scratching."

The uncle's voice came from a doorway beside the foot of the bed.

"Come and eat."

The boy found clothes stacked on a chair and put them on. Everything was blue and a little too big. Rafferty didn't think he had anything at home to wear that was blue except socks. These blue socks and sweater were especially bulky, but warm. This was the first time he remembered having warm feet since the hatch.

Now, sitting at the cold grave five years later, Rafferty remembered that as the last time he had had milk from a refrigerator.

"This is the last of the bacon," Uncle had told him. "Those other pigs won't be ready to put down yet for another month."

Uncle had been right. That was the last time he'd had bacon, too, but this year . . .

"Bacon this year, buddy," Uncle had said, but Rafferty didn't know how to get the bacon out of the pigs. In the five years since that morning at his uncle's table he'd learned to eat that meal over and over in his mind. Then he'd learned not to.

Verna's brother sat across the table from Rafferty that morning and sipped his coffee. He was balding, and when he sipped coffee the furrows in his brow opened and closed in contrast to the steadiness of those blue eyes. Uncle was always grinning. Rafferty knew that pretty soon he was going to have to talk. His plate was almost empty.

"What's your name?" the uncle asked.

"Rafferty." He tried to get his throat to swallow a mouthful of dry fried potatoes. "What's yours?"

The uncle frowned. "I thought you knew it," he said. "You called my name when I found the car. It's Henry. Call me Uncle Henry."

Rafferty blushed.

"I didn't say Henry," he said. "I said *hungry.*"

Henry laughed without adjusting his grin much and said, "Well, then call me 'Uncle Hungry.' There's going to be a lot of it going around."

A week later, the first raiders came through. Uncle Hungry woke him up with a hand over his mouth, grabbed up some clothes and blankets and led him into the dirt basement. He slid aside something that looked like a piece of the furnace and he put Rafferty into a tunnel.

"Crawl ahead," he whispered. "Stop when you get to an open space."

From upstairs they heard the splintering of cupboards and shelves, the heavy thump of bootheels, curses. Rafferty heard Uncle Hungry close the tunnel behind them, heard him stop several times. The boy picked his way through roots and fallen-in chunks of sharp rock. Suddenly the tunnel opened up on both sides. When the uncle caught up with him he switched on a red flashlight. Rafferty stared at the grotesque mechanical creature that squatted in the middle of the room.

Uncle nudged him out of the way and stepped over to a case of bottles and wedged the flashlight into some wing-colored coils rising out of the creature's head. Then he jammed a roll of pink stuff into the opening they'd just crawled through. The uncle sat in one of two overstuffed chairs and waved Rafferty towards the other. They sat inside a huge underground room full of sacks, bottles, crates and their two chairs.

The uncle noticed his interest in the creature in the center of the room.

"It's a big cooking-pot," Uncle said. "Called a 'still.' It cooks cereal, from those bags."

He pointed to some sacks stacked on a board beside him. Rafferty tried to imagine how many bowls of cereal you could cook in that still, and where you might find that many people at breakfast.

"Nobody can find us here," Uncle told him. "We'll hide out here until they're gone."

The room with the still was the quietest place that Rafferty had ever known. He heard all of his own breaths, and all of Uncle Hungry's. Uncle's stomach gurgled every few minutes and sounded like a conver sation in another room.

"We have plenty of batteries," Uncle said. "We have a water faucet. Lots of cereal and sugar but no way to cook it without getting caught."

We, Rafferty thought. *He said that* we *have plenty of batteries!*

He didn't know how long he slept that first night in the still, but he remembered being so hungry when he woke up that his stomach cramped when he took a drink of cold water. They couldn't leave yet, the raiders were camped in the house.

"We can get out if we have to," Uncle said. "This other tunnel comes up between the manure pile and the barn. But then we'd just have to hide, so we might as well hide here, since we're already here and as safe as we'll get."

He stirred a couple of spoonfuls of sugar into the water.

"Here," Uncle said. "Drink it, now. It'll stop the cramps."

Uncle Hungry figured that they hid in the still for fifty-one days, living on that sugar and water and grain. Another party of raiders killed the first bunch, stripped them, carried off all the rest of the food. It was late summer when they came out of the ground, and Rafferty couldn't tell where the sky and the earth left off because of the dust.

In fifty-one days in the still, Uncle Hungry taught Rafferty letters and spelling, reading, numbers and counting money up to $11.06. Rafferty taught him the rope-skipping song, the song about stars, and a trick for getting gum out of his hair. A couple of times a day each of them would pull the insulation aside and crawl halfway back up the tunnel to listen in a pipe that led to the kitchen. Farther up the tunnel, about a dozen feet from the house, was a trap that would collapse that half of the tunnel if anybody touched it. Uncle told him how to unhook it, but Rafferty didn't ever go up any farther than the pipe.

They traded stories and, finally, secrets. Rafferty told him about eating the bugs. The uncle laughed and said, "You won't be the last one that eats bugs, you'll see." Uncle didn't make fun of him for eating the bugs. He asked a lot of questions about them, including how they tasted.

"Like corn dogs," Rafferty said. But it wasn't really true. He couldn't remember how they tasted, he just remembered trying to think they were corn dogs.

Then the uncle told his story. Rafferty didn't know what to do when a man cried so he sat still, curled up in his dirt-caked chair.

"Verna and I, we had a brother," Uncle said. "He was the oldest. There was Floyd, then me, then Verna. We were three years apart."

Uncle talked in the low whisper that they'd developed down there in the still. He cleared his throat and coughed.

"Floyd worked in the city for sixteen years. He started drinking. When he disappeared for the first time, this is where I found him. My father built this still. I run it when I can't get work, but I don't drink it myself. The last time I found my brother, I found him here. He was drunk and had a rifle with him. I figured he might be down here if he was on a toot, and I was right. He sat here up against the still holding the rifle across his chest and when I saw that, I was scared. I thought if he was drunk he might shoot me, and I could see he was drunk. I was so *scared* . . . ."

The uncle was a little shaky and his voice squeaked when he tried to start talking again.

"I said to him, 'Floyd, let me take that back up to the house for you.' He wouldn't look at me. Kept looking off at the ground. Finally he said, 'Henry, you go back to the house now.' Then I knew what he was going to do. I waited there where the tunnel opens in, I don't know how long, just feeling the jump of my heart make my knees shake. Then I backed up the tunnel and was dusting myself off when I heard the shot. He was dead before I got back in there. And something about that really made me mad. I was thirty-two years old. He should've given me the rifle and done it another time. Or shot himself while I was looking. But his way I was a part of it because I didn't stop him. I *couldn't* stop him. I was *scared*. . . ."

That had been their twentieth day, and it was also the day that the raiders shot each other in a fight. There were seven, then five; then there came the priests who killed the five and stole the food.

When the uncle and Rafferty finally surfaced that hot summer day, when they quit blinking back the insistent sting of the sun, they pointed out to each other the local variations on death.

There was no sign of vegetation. The animals that lived were nearly dead. Starved and spooky, two thin Angus stumbled across the driveway, most of the hair missing from their hides. Featherless chicken carcasses littered the yard, stinking up the afternoon. Some had been eaten by something else. The bugs were around, but not so many. Uncle pointed to a dead calf covered with the things.

"They ate all the greenery. Now they've got a taste for hair and hooves. Looks like they're fond of paint."

The house and barn, the outbuildings and the fence around the pigpen all wore the same gray expression.

The uncle stood in the middle of the dusty drive, hand shading his eyes. He had fifty-one days of dirt packed into his shirt, pants, hair and skin. Later Uncle showed Rafferty a picture of some stunned miners after a cave-in and they looked just the same. Blinking in blackface, white around the eyeballs and lips too pink, the uncle brought his hand down and settled it on Rafferty's head.

"Let's wash up," he said. "If the pump's not working there's always the spring. Then we better figure out a recipe for those goddam bugs."

Figuring out recipes was easy. The hard part was figuring how to catch and keep a couple of tons of dead bugs. They dried the bugs under screens in the yard, then ground them into a meal that made "soup, cakes or steaks," as Uncle Hungry put it. They filled everything on the place that could be converted into a container. For as long as the electricity held out, which was most of the following year, they had no trouble catching bagfuls of the things. Uncle put up a chicken-wire fence on stilts and covered the top with more chicken-wire. He hooked this up to the house wires and whenever a cloud of the pretty bronze things came through on the wind he touched two wires together. Bugs dropped by the thousands as they were electrocuted on the wire.

Rafferty and the uncle would go outside and shovel the catch out onto the drying tables they'd made. It was Rafferty's job to keep away the birds and turn over the bugs.

After two years, raids on the place pretty much stopped but the uncle was careful with smoke and fires. He showed Rafferty how to make fires, how to tell what animal left tracks and where it was headed, where it had been and why.

After they got out that first time, that August afternoon, Rafferty and Uncle Hungry never moved back into the house. They salvaged what they could from the broken walls and they built up the underground room with the still. The uncle piped in spring water beside the well water, and they hid down there two more times in five years, but they were ready. Both times, they nearly got caught, but Rafferty didn't want to think about those times right now.

The sun slipped a shoulder through the clouds and the crow chattered to itself. Rafferty realized that he and the uncle could go days without saying anything more than "Morning." "Catch anything?" "Find anything?" "Yep." "Nope."

With just a hint of wind and mutters of his restless crow in his ears, Rafferty felt something cold flip-flop inside his stomach. It was like that certain point in hunger, the point of reflex that made him gnash down that first bug, the juicy one that tormented his face. His mind kept replaying the shake in Uncle's voice that time underground when he said, "I was so *scared* . . . ."

Rafferty looked up at the loft window near the top of the barn wall, where Uncle Hungry's green stocking cap perched the sill.

What was he doing in that window? Rafferty thought.

The sound of the thought was a shout, not a wonder. He tried to swallow around the strangle in his throat.

"Didn't he know he could fall?" he asked the crow.

A shift of cloud shut out the sun and the crow ruffled its feathers. The boy Rafferty eyed both horizons of the road: sunrise and sunset. He spoke to the one yellow crocus beside the barn.

"Didn't he know he could fall?"

Rafferty was sure, by the shake in his voice, that he was scared.

2

Sunday Drive

A dead-end back road not far from here
drops the heavy lid of shadow down behind you
and there's no turning back.

You learn to live there
and give your private names
to mushrooms, berries, and the wind.

That town at the beginning of the road
was a movie you saw the end of once.
And the people you know there?
And their faces?

Yes, turn back to your lean-to
and the gentle pulse of your fire.
Turn that new name for *nothing*
over and over in your mind.

Sitting Home

Rain, and rain again.
This drizzle grows nothing but distance.

Alder and willow yellow early this year.
Nighthawks lose out to winter and somewhere
out there at least one black hole motions
come here come here to us, the alders, the nighthawks

and all these fragments of light and shimmer
that we call "Now."

Breathe deep this damp distance, this speeding blackness
that holds us, without touching, together.

The Something

Something to spite the sun is coming to get us.
Ripley Schemm

The something was coming has gone
and all our chickens roost in the branches of eclipse.

The body that blocks our sun is nothing.
This cone of shade, this penumbra
triggers the bats and crawly things
and long, terrifying dreams.

I owe my cold sweat to the something
that spites the sun
and nothing so easy as cloud
nothing so brief as the regular passage of moons
washes the beauty out of my eyes, and gone.

Roosters mark the end of this abnormal night
out of their own inherent dimness, not joy.
Not joy like the sudden high dancing of tribes
or the thankful turn of some farmer's face
upward to the warm.

Or my private joy, here, wringing out
what light I can from memory
finishing this dark poem with hope.

A Dream In Five Faces

Sleep with a mouthful of blood.
Annie Dillard

Even in my dreams you bring me chamomile tea
to stop these late-night mutterings, twisting sheets
and this terror that sweats its grease between us.

Your hands, a steaming question,
uncurl from the cup.

The stain there, where you spilled it,
that could have been ours.

*

We meet at dusk on an old back porch,
the slant roof stoops us over a box of puppies.
We reach out to rub their fat bellies—
our cold hands touch, touch again.

Our bodies and eyes speak in distances:
Snow fields, telephone lines hung with ice
and the curled lip of a dog frozen gray in the ditch.

But these, our hands, tumble over themselves
aglow in this squirm of lives and blind pups.

*

Remember me? I am yours.
When you left, you left me this.

Mother, you hand me a key, a small one.

I forget what it unlocks.
It sticks to my fingers
while you, beloved stranger, skip away.

Dynamite caps in a red shirt pocket
blew the laundry apart.
You stayed on, red-knuckled and vomiting,
folded hot sheets by the hundred.

Your overtime bought me gloves
to cushion my blisters in the cannery.

Tonight you offer me another new pair
but you turn your face aside.

This time I say *Thank you,* and wake myself.

           *

The shot, as always, flashes from the left.
It kicks me sideways into the road
and down, twitching, all circuits cut.

There are no questions.

Just my face cold on the back of my arm
veins and arteries folding one by one
and, again, this useless blood clots black on my teeth.

Living Will

Burn me.
Pay the fine, stand aside and sift me through wind.

Wish I could see myself flake down
over ferns and moss, backs of beetles and crumbling rock.
I never looked better.

Remember my eyes to the sun.
My daughter, hold her tight as earth.

Look up these certain women.
Be discreet as the blush I never had.
It's all right. Their touch, like me, is gone.

A mouthful of ash and dust in the corners
that's what I own.
Peddle them if you can.

If you are my wife, sorry.
I hoard no secret wealth.

Last Rites

*The immortal being issues from something humble and
forgotten, indeed, from a wholly improbable source.*

C. G. Jung

1.
_____

𓇋𓎡𓃀𓋹

I have become alive.

He holds his eyes in his hands
and lifts them slowly, slowly.
All the bones of the heavens,
all the dried and whitened lives
that were fathers, mothers and gods
chatter in the face of this new chill.
The skies lower.
Stars on this side of night
hide themselves and tremble.
His eyes rise watery and full
and assume their places.
His heart is an oar creaking through the dark.

_____

*Here begin the testimonies of coming forth
by day, the praiseful, glorifying songs.*

The shuffling step that approaches is his own.
Even before the scented breath
and the strong familiar hand reach him
he whispers his name through the hollow calm
between waves and gusts of wind.
A clap of hands on his shoulders,

name on his tongue:
the sweet close breath licks his face.
The eyes of his Shadow are whole.
They fix on his heart
and become his eyes.
He faces a glow in the East.

You shall not imprison my soul.

He snuffs the breeze, bends
and gulps from the stream at his feet.
The true name of the waters is his.
Shadow on his left and boat on his right,
he steps into the current.
His heart unfurls and fills
and begins its ancient journey.
He has no words.
The stream slips North,
a song in the first gray light.
A whiff of fresh bread across the water
and that boat drifting from the right brings the sun.

Behold, I inherit eternity, everlastingness.

2.

I am pure.

A priest on the boat waves a serpent,
sings a spell, old as light:
   Your spirit is Heron.
   Your great wings stretch and bank.
   Your neck sleeks out at the sun.
   Your eyes,
   your great black eyes
   glitter with the sweat of night itself. . .
The feet of his Shadow, numb in the stream,
tingle with the cadence and dream-like sway
of priest and rippling serpent.
At last his deserted mouth opens.

𓏜𓀁𓏏𓅱𓀀𓏏𓏏𓍿𓂋𓏛𓈖𓏥𓄿𓏏𓇋𓏤𓂋𓏛

Leave me the sweet breath of your nostrils.
I embrace the great throne.

His words draw the boat like a lover,
and the light of their power warms the earth.
The priest offers bread, body and gift of the sun,
loaf of truth.
And the twelve behind the priest
(attendants and scribes, steersman)
bring parcels of dried fishes and wine.
He steps to the boat, and boards.
They make way for his strength and his darkness.
Behind him the priest lifts a golden balance.

35

His Shadow eats quietly of the sun,
breathless lotus in the loaf of truth.

---

*Oh, you who hand out cakes and ale to saints in the house of Osiris,
hand them out twice a day.*

The dog-faced priest presents him a necklace;
in its center shines a pale green stone.
The touch of the stone to his chest
rattles across his empty ribs.
Stone in hand, he faces the priest:
> *Let me eat.*
> *Let me have my mouth to speak, my legs to walk.*
> *Let me have my arms to overthrow my enemies.*
> *Let me rise.*
> *Let my dark goddess fly to me.*

He pauses, closes his eyes:
> *I am master of my heart.*

I am the Lord of Hearts, slayer of the heart-jar.

3.

I have stopped no water that should flow.

A hawk is mother to his heart.
It hatches in his chest and rustles through his blood.
His eyes bear the first signs:
red-rimmed, golden, privy to the slightest movement.
This heart cannot be stolen, snatched away,
driven out like a thief from the tomb
or a name from an unholy spirit.
A light wind snaps at the sail
and the great boat bears west.
He signals the blackness between the mountains
that his words are back, his power is whole
and the dark is his next harbor.

Heart of my mother, heart of my mother.
Heart-box of my breath upon the earth.

The shore of his darkness opens.
Pale mouths flop on the banks
open as night they screech and beg,
and their empty eyes open
on his face, wide as sunrise on spring wheat.
He breathes the light of his mane on their heads.
The sun rises in their flesh, slow as worms.
The hollows of their eyes are crocus
that bloom in his leathery hands.
He passes them bread

and bowls of clear water from the East.
Behind the thrash of their hunger, his black country.

Let not my body become worms, deliver me as you delivered yourself.

He sets his sails for the foothills.
The priest and attendants, the steersman
sing the songs of ending and memorize their names.
His boat rides the rocks and gravel high and smooth as a swan.
The sun, lodged on the mast above him,
lights no more than the decks at his feet
and his brown, shaggy face.
The darkness parts before them like high thick grass
and closes behind them like stone.
The light in his chest and the eyes of his Shadow
creep through the mountains ahead.
Beside him, on the rail, an owl.

Greetings, Spirit, you mighty one of terror. Behold how I come to you. I see you. I have crossed the great unknown.

4.

𓀀𓄿𓏭𓏭𓏏𓆓

     Take me.
The woman's voice brushes his ear
quickens the hawk of his heart.
She hops to his arm, then shoulder
and whispers: *Open your hands and your ears.*
He strokes her feathers,
and they become hair, ear, jaw, mouth:
     In the mountains hangs a figure,
     a silver hand pointing down.
     It keeps the names of all who see it;
     it keeps the light itself.
Footsteps and cries of terror brush them in the night.

𓄿𓂧𓀭

Take me.

The sun floats from the mast,
settles above his head and brightens.
He stares heavily into the dark
sees the mountain rise rock by rock
sees the deep canyons scarring its face
and the brittle barrens of unweathered stone.
That distant hand fills with the light of the sun,
glistens a cold hard blue.
He closes his eyes, lifts his arms
and pulls the fading sun to his chest.

He whispers his name, strong as life,
and a melt of bright silver lights the earth.

I have conquered every lock in heaven and earth.

He opens his eyes and he is light.
He returns the sun to the mast,
and the bow of the boat crests the mountain.
The owl-woman stands beside him, sleek.
The priest, attendants and steersman slip out of hatches
and take their places on deck.
He smiles at their pale faces
and sweeps his heavy arm before them.
As they sail down the mountain,
all of the world ahead stretches wide and green.
He throws back his shaggy head and sings:
  I am pure I am pure I am pure

---

*I am the embodied Spirit, I am the Spirit's soul. I have all
that I need. I salute the gods and every Spirit's soul.*

  for LaVerne

Beloved mother, deceased.

3

Letter From The Lost Notebooks

for Frank Herbert

Starting from where the road forks, we lose time
and we lose the lives that might have followed us here.
We lock our memories in the car, leave the keys on the muffler
and begin the slow drizzling climb (it always rains
here in the valley) to the flatlands somewhere near the top.
Notice, as we climb, whole huckleberry bushes stripped
of leaves and limbs. Bear, stoking up for winter.
You notice, too, that by switching back on ourselves
we walk quite a way and make very little ground.
If making ground is what you're after
you wouldn't have come this far.

If you came here with a lover or a friend, don't be surprised
if you are now alone. These things happen up here.

You reach the high flatlands in late afternoon.
The rain settles into haze and drops itself, patch by patch,
into the valleys and crannies below. This high up
there is never a hurry, so look over the meadow and watch,
as the sky clears for sundown, how those old boulders sit
hunched and waiting. Listen.

The wind scribbles something slight on their faces.
Sleep out there tonight, among them, and know
that the dreams they send may be more than you can wake up from.

Walking the Whitman Mission

Step east, into their shadows.
Stand with cottonwoods at your back
and hold your breath as they hold theirs.

Listen for screams stuttering
through the crumbling memories of stones.

Kneel here between the ruts
push your hand deep into mud.
Your pulse echoes the westering throb
of wheels and oxen, axes.

Winds off the Blue Mountains
ripple ryegrass, your hair
a thin harvest of faces in a pond.

Turn your back to the sentry on the hill.
He strikes the air with feathers
and drums out the fever in his eyes.
Behind him, a clatter of dried bones
scatters like wings.

One magpie struts and pokes
at bright red splashes in the leaves.

The mud on your hand flakes off.
you leave your breath here
a white feather twirling in clean winter air.

The Center

What is truth?
    Pilate

A talking skull on the tip of a spear
faces west, shrieks with the night wind:

If they do these things in a green tree,
what shall they do in a dry?

A one-eyed dog whines below,
licks the sores of any beggar.
These two, and a cracked lamp
keep watch in the square.

We are shadows in our own homes,
we flicker like black tongues
behind curtains and our plank doors.

If they do these things in a green tree,
what shall they do in a dry?

There are no children here.
The smooth path around the skull
wears deeper every year,
the sand in the center grows darker.

We would leave
but there are so few of us
and the distance from the center is so great.

from *Jaguar*

Progress is not immediate ease, well-being and peace. It is not rest. It is not even, directly, virtue. Essentially Progress is a force, and the most dangerous of forces. . . .
                    Pierre Teilhard de Chardin, *The Future of Man*

EDDIE Reyes was a quiet boy even before the earthquake and the explosion downtown. People spoke in those days of his mother's blue eyes that he got to spite his dark skin, and the absence of his father, but the real talk later always came down to the earthquake or the explosion. What they whispered of in this quiet valley was Eddie's mother, and what he had done to her, and though this with his mother was an equally long time ago, it clearly had changed his life.

Dark-skinned Eddie and his pale-skinned mother lived with her parents just a few blocks from the Daffodil Laundry, a sprawling brick building behind the tracks that split the valley into equal measures of town and farm. His father had been run over by a jeep while waiting for a flight home from the war. Eddie never met him, but he could pick him out in the picture of hard-eyed men lined up under the wing of their bomber.

Six men stood with their legs apart and their arms folded in their leather jackets. Eddie's dad was the only dark-faced man in the group. He wore his hat tilted back and a cigarette drooped from the corner of his mouth. Painted on the side of the plane were four rows of bombs to show the missions they'd survived. Eddie counted sixty-two.

Every day after Eddie became five, his grandfather walked him the three blocks to the cafe next door to the laundry. There they would meet his mother for a soda while she took her break. His mother was a small, thin-faced woman who laughed a lot and Eddie remembered that even though she was skinny she was always sweating from the heat of her machine.

46

She worked a machine she called "the mangle" that steam-pressed things between a pair of huge canvas lips. Sometimes she let him work the foot pedal while she set the creases. When the mangle responded, it hissed like a small locomotive coming to a stop right in front of him. Hot. Very, very hot.

Something about sirens and a still, hot day in spring would fix Eddie Reyes like a dead bug to a board for the rest of his life. It started with the earthquake that spring when he was almost six.

Eddie sat on the sidewalk taking a wind-up clock apart while his cousin drew around him with colored chalk. Eddie liked the feel of taking things apart and putting them together, even when he was five. His grandfather made him a small toolbox of his own and it was his grandfather who gave him the clock. Suddenly, one of the gears that he'd set aside, the brass one with the axle through it, began turning all by itself in the middle of the pavement.

Eddie and his cousin watched amazed as the colored swirls of chalk bulged up with the rest of the sidewalk and then burst apart. The long sidewalk behind his cousin shook itself out like a rug and the street broke into huge chunks of concrete. The scrape of buckling concrete and deep-throated groans of unseated rock shook suddenly back and forth: *Bam-bam Bam-bam.* Then a hiatus of stillness burst in one long rip of twisted lumber and the crumple of nearby walls.

Eddie thought it was like someone picked up the earth and shook it like an old shirt, then tore it apart.

Neighbors ran from their houses into the shattered street, shouting names and warnings. Some screamed. Some dusted themselves off and looked at the sky, others looked at parts of themselves to be sure they were still alive.

"Power lines here, watch out!"

"Gas . . . !"

Some stumbled out squinty and stunned, as though seeing the sun for the first time. Mrs. Brown, when she found her husband underneath the fallen wires, screamed in fright and grief. Some screamed names of children that Eddie knew. More than once he heard his own name, and his cousin's. Neither of them moved and he saw that her eyes watched over his shoulder as he watched over hers. He heard her wet breathing, the *sniff* at her runny nose.

Now the clear air carried shouts of pain, and when he was sure the earth would stay still he slowly stood up. He wanted to run to his mother at her work, and he looked up the street towards the laundry.

Mrs. Gratzer grabbed Eddie and his cousin. She gasped, "Oh you poor kids. You poor kids. You must be scared to death."

She was huge, and had each of them tucked under an arm like bags of grain. Eddie couldn't breathe because of her grip and the press of her sweaty apron against his face. He hadn't had time to be scared yet, but he was starting to get that feeling in his stomach, that fast-elevator feeling that meant big trouble.

Mrs. Gratzer teetered in the doorway as she toed the screen door with her foot. The explosion from downtown pushed the three of them over in a heap. It was more of a feeling than a sound, a sudden punch in his lungs that popped his ears and took his breath away. Eddie landed on top of Mrs. Gratzer and his cousin started crying from underneath.

"Jesus, Mary and Joseph," she said.

When Eddie followed the course her gaze took he saw the huge boil of black smoke from downtown sniffing the street towards them. Things in the middle of it *pop-pop-popped* like fireworks. A fountain of fire burst through the smoke high into the sky.

"Mom."

He remembered later that he simply said her name just like that and his emotions went completely blank. His body dodged Mrs. Gratzer's grab by itself and scrambled through the rubble up the street.

Everything changed so much with the smoke and with buildings spilled into the pavement and the pavement broken that Eddie almost got lost. He tripped over one of the railroad tracks, then followed it to what used to be the back door of the laundry. Most of the building was gone. Bricks and broken glass littered the street and everywhere people dug into them and shouted names. The center of the laundry was a huge ball of fire, unaffected by the spray from all the broken pipes.

Standing there that day, staring at the rubble, he was reminded of the mangle because of the loud hiss of steam coming from everywhere, not quite loud enough to drown out the screams. The mangle had been attached to the wall that was now gone.

Wide-eyed firefighters dragged hoses through the streetful of brick chunks and glass to hook up to hydrants that didn't work. Shreds of charred sheets and blackened rags of pillowcases tumbled in the wind that started up with the fire. Everyone seemed so pale.

"Mom!" Eddie hollered. "Mom!"

One of the women from the front office, Eleanor, who wore the glittery pins, pulled him from the middle of the street to what was left of the sidewalk. Her glasses were gone and her hair on one side was melted to her head in a clump.

"Eddie, your momma's not here. Some people just carried her and Robert and Nell over to the hospital. Wait here with me for your grandpa . . . ."

Eddie twisted loose and splashed through the flooded alley to the street, crowded with people making their way to the wreckage of the laundry. He ran through the front door of the Alber's Feed Store and out the back, which put him at the back door of the hospital. It was the same hospital where he'd been born, where his mother had been born. He heard shouts from in there, and screams, and the sound of something metal crashing to the floor.

Inside the back door a pasty-faced nurse snatched his arm and hissed, "Don't you run in here. Now you get right back outside."

"My mom . . . ," he said, and tried to twist free but it didn't work this time. No matter how he moved she knew how to hold him. She pushed the back door open with her hip.

"I want my Mom!"

A pair of heavy double doors slapped open in the hallway behind them. The nurse pulled him aside, but not before he caught a glimpse of Robert, the retarded janitor, who held his bandaged hands away from the bulky bandages on his chest. His lips and nose were covered with little white pads. He cried in little howls. In the quick slap of the doors Eddie heard people hurrying in there, heard the clatter of steel against steel.

The nurse pulled him back through the door then guided him down the hallway without loosening her grip.

"Someone in the front can help you," she said. "We're too busy back here and you shouldn't be in here, anyway. What's your name?"

"Eddie Reyes," he said.

They rounded the hallway turn and he saw his grandfather at the nurses' desk, at the front of a mob of people, wringing his old felt hat. His grandfather didn't say anything. His stare made Eddie feel smaller every step he took.

"They want us to go to the waiting room," his grandpa said. "It'll be awhile yet before they know . . ."

He didn't finish.

"Before they know what?" Eddie asked.

His grandfather's huge hand pressed against his shoulder blades, the other held the waiting-room door open. Eddie ducked under. The place smelled of coffee and cigarette smoke. All around the walls, people sat on benches and cried or read magazines. The room was so full he could barely breathe, and people kept coming in.

Eddie's mother lived through that day, the next, and the next. The hospital wouldn't allow him to see her, and his grandfather said that she would be there for a long time. It scared him that they didn't tell him anything except that his mother would be all right. In their private glances between each other, Eddie could see that his grandparents didn't believe it. And when one or both of them came back from the hospital, they whispered between each other and they didn't talk with him.

Eddie walked every day through the Alber's Feed Store and out the back. From there he could see her room, her window, and sometimes the curtains moved. He thought then that she waved, and he always waved back.

For three months, she lay up in that old building. The ivy outside turned from scraggly thin ropes to a lush green cover that shaded many of the windows up to the third floor. His mother was up there, her hands a vapor and her face a vague memory in the bathroom mirror.

One day, one of the nurses came out to make him go away.

"What are you doing out here?"

He didn't answer.

"You come here to see somebody, don't you? Is it your brother?"

"My mother."

"Oh, your *mother*. . . ."

Third floor, he thought, *the window next to the rusty ladder.*

He said nothing.

"You know, there are other sick people here. They don't like it when people look in their windows."

He ran down to the park and stayed there until the gulls screamed upriver to the dump. He was hungry when he got to his grandparents' place. They fed him in quiet, as usual. The kitchen smelled like that nurse, and later his cold sheets tightened on him like her hand.

He lay there as wide-eyed as his pet rabbit, thinking about his mom, about the whispers and rumors. He had heard that she didn't have any hands or face anymore, but he didn't think it was true because he couldn't imagine it, and as long as he couldn't imagine it, it couldn't be true.

Eddie made people uncomfortable because he asked to see her every day. He didn't belong anywhere, anymore, it seemed. Kid games seemed like kid games to him, now. He belonged with his mother, he decided, and he decided he would see her on his birthday. That was five days away.

That night, and every night for the next five nights, Eddie dreamed of the sidewalk and the road breaking up in front of him, and of a boy his own age watching it all in a blue halo from the other side, the *under*side.

In his dreams the sidewalk and the road tilted up to become a wall. When they split apart and the chunks rained down, the crack that was left open was an opening to another world. It was a long way off, like a tunnel, but Eddie saw light through it, blue light and another face looking back at him.

The boy at the end of the tunnel was more a shadow than a boy, but Eddie felt that this was his friend, his best friend, something he'd never had before. In the dreams, when he tried to get a look at the boy, the shadow always turned away, but not without a hesitation, and a look back over his shoulder.

"What's your name?" Eddie hollered through the crack in one dream, but it came out a dry croak that woke him up, and he didn't catch the answer.

*

If you have not seen the day of revolution in a small town where all know all in the town and always have known all, you have seen nothing. . . .
Ernest Hemingway, *For Whom the Bell Tolls*

THE valley was small, lush, crowded against the mountain by the monster city downriver. Farmers in the valley supported a small town on berries, beans and flower bulbs. Like any small town of any language, nearly everything about anyone was known by everyone. Invisibility, even for a quiet child like Eddie Reyes, was out of the question.

A clerk in the feed store watched every day as Eddie walked in the front door, past the brooder full of baby chicks, and out the open double doors in the back. Some days, Eddie bought small red salt licks for his rabbits, sometimes a bag of oats, but usually he simply walked through. The clerk never asked about his mother, and Eddie never brought it up.

The clerk, Weldon, was one of the few men in town with a beard. It was blond, broad and bushy. Weldon was the tallest man Eddie had ever seen. He was strong enough to throw feed sacks and hay bales into trucks all day without sweating or slowing down. Many men made the feed store their base of gossip and conversation, but Weldon never joined in. He wasn't sullen, he was always busy and simply ignored them while they had their coffee at his counter or on his hay bales. Weldon was another mystery of the valley, one who smiled, worked hard and kept to himself. He had been arrested once for poaching deer out of season with a flintlock, and some called him "Mountain Man" after that, but not to his face.

Sometimes, when Eddie hurried through the store and their glances met, Weldon would nod and then shuffle some papers, stack something or pick up his broom. Eddie was sure that Weldon could reach the rusty fire escape ladder that zig-zagged behind the ivy and up the back wall of the hospital to his mother's window.

His birthday dawned with the second Friday in June, and Eddie waited outside the feed store for Weldon to open up. The morning stayed gray, and the clouds squeezed a slow drizzle onto the shoulders of the town. The black rabbit under Eddie's coat squirmed against his ribs. It wasn't weaned yet, but it knew Eddie well enough not to struggle when he picked it up. He talked to the rabbit every day, because he had nobody else to talk to.

A trickle of rain slipped down the back of his collar. Eddie shrugged and pressed himself further back into the shallow doorway. The loose fender of Weldon's pickup rattled as it made the turn.

"He's coming," Eddie said.

The rabbit said nothing.

"Morning," was all Weldon said.

Weldon glanced at Eddie a couple of times while he worked the key into the old lock. He waited for Eddie to step aside, then unlocked the door. It was almost a half hour early, so he left the sign in the door that said "Closed."

Weldon fussed with his big coffee machine while Eddie leaned against the counter and petted the rabbit under his coat. Eddie was nervous, now, and so was the rabbit. It was breathing faster, and it poked its busy nose further under his armpit.

Weldon put the lid on the urn, plugged it in and slid it to the corner of the counter beside Eddie. Then he waited. Eddie felt him waiting and when he finally glanced up Weldon's eyebrows rose as if to ask, "Well?"

"I need some help," Eddie blurted. His bottom front teeth weren't quite grown back enough to stop a slight lisp.

Weldon smiled, and without lowering his huge, bushy eyebrows he asked, "Help with what?"

"That fire escape," Eddie said, and he nodded towards the back of the store, towards the hospital. Weldon didn't seem surprised.

"Now, in the daylight?"

"It's my birthday."

The rabbit scrambled a little to turn itself around. Weldon's glance flicked to the front of Eddie's coat, back to his eyes.

"If we're going to do it, let's do it now," Weldon said. It came out as a long sigh. Weldon was already headed for the rear doors and Eddie hurried to keep up.

The big man jumped up, grabbed the lowest rung, and pulled. He dropped to the ground, but the ladder hadn't budged. Weldon jumped up again and got a better grip this time. He bounced himself on it twice and let go.

"Jesus," he said. His face was red and he was breathing hard. Weldon looked up and down the alley between the buildings, then patted Eddie on the back.

"Are you *sure* you have to go this way?"

Eddie nodded. "They won't let me in. You have to be fourteen."

Weldon mumbled something into his beard.

"What?"

"Nothing. Come on."

Eddie followed Weldon back to the feed store. Weldon took another key from his mass of keys and opened up the coke machine. He unclicked the mechanism and a bottle of coke dropped out. He put the machine back together, like a refrigerator, and opened the bottle. He offered it to Eddie and Eddie took a sip. He couldn't tip the bottle up without dropping the rabbit out from under his arm, so all he could get was a sip.

Weldon took a swallow, then said, "Watch this."

This time when he jumped, he grabbed the rung with his left hand and held the coke in his right. He shook up the bottle with his thumb over the top, then sprayed the rest of the coke into the hinge of the ladder. He tossed the empty to Eddie, got a good grip and bounced it a couple more times. The rusty ramp unkinked itself with a sharp screech. It was slow going, and not at all as quiet as Eddie had hoped.

Weldon was sweating pretty hard. Eddie had seen him work hard in the feed store and this was the first time he'd seen him sweat. Weldon bounced on it again but it wouldn't come down all the way.

"Can you jump and reach that now?" Weldon asked. He was trying to talk and catch his breath at the same time.

Eddie stood underneath and the tips of his right fingers almost touched the rung. He nodded.

"Yes."

He looked both ways, there was still no one in the alley. Someone out front of the feed store was pounding for Weldon to let him in.

"What about this?" Weldon asked. He patted the bulge in Eddie's jacket where the rabbit hid. Without waiting for an answer, Weldon picked Eddie up and set him on the fire escape.

"Thanks," Eddie said.

"Happy birthday," Weldon said. "Good luck."

He walked back inside the store.

Eddie didn't like the gratings under the steps of the fire escape. He could see clear through to the ground and it seemed a long way down already. He worked his way up the three floors through the ivy to his mother's window, trying to keep the rabbit calm against the thrash of his heart in his chest.

He spent a minute with his eyes closed, catching his breath. Through the ivy he glimpsed the shadow of a boy his own age dodge down the alleyway towards the mill. The lumber mill on the next block was three blocks long and they grazed sheep among the stacks of lumber. His glimpse of the boy showed him only someone his own age and size, someone like the boy in his dreams.

Rafferty.

The name from inside his head sounded perfect. This shadow had skirted him for awhile now, it had even skipped through the edges of his dreams. In the last dream, Eddie looked down on the shadow-boy from the gnarled branch of a yew. From where he perched, Eddie could see the boy hiding down there, and someone circled towards him in the grass. Eddie looked down from the tree to see himself reflected in brown lakewater: he was a crow. He shook his wings out to make sure. His heart was beating awfully fast, and whatever it was nearly had the boy.

Rafferty.

Again, the name had awakened him from a sweaty sleep, but Eddie had barked it in the brusque vernacular of a crow. Now he scanned the sky and treetops. There were crows, all right, but they all stayed put. The trees swayed, and a bit of a headache made him squint even though it was too cloudy for glare.

When he heard voices in the back of the feed store he raised his mother's window and stepped through, between the curtains.

Eddie's mother must have heard the window, because as he slung one leg over the sill she gave out a little cry of surprise. She had already partly covered herself with the sheet she gathered between her stumps. A white patch covered one of her eyes. All he could really see of her the way she huddled into her sheet was her one blue eye surrounded by a swirl of pink scars to the top of her head where her hairline began.

Eddie's rabbit squirmed against his ribs.

His mother made that cry again and he realized it was his name. She glanced at the blue curtain that separated her bed from the rest of the room. It was closed. Eddie heard snoring from somewhere on the other side. His mother's blanket shifted, and on her patched-eye side her ear looked like a melted flowerbud.

He pulled his other leg over and scooted off the sill into the room.

"Eddie," she whispered, and hunched the blanket higher, "I don't want you to see."

She lowered her head and he thought she would tell him to leave.

Then she sighed, and whispered, "But I've wanted to see you so *much.*"

She talked through a tight throat, and her shoulders shook. She cleared her throat and lowered the sheet so that Eddie could see her eye.

"It's your birthday and you were born right here, downstairs. . . ."

She shifted herself over on her bed and patted the cover beside her. He listened, before he moved, for sounds of anybody in the hallway, but it was quiet.

"Six," she whispered. "You're six and you're such a little man already."

She was shivering but he only noticed it after he sat on the bed beside her. This close, there was a very strong smell that he didn't like, and the rabbit didn't like it either because it started scrambling under his jacket until it got out and onto the bed. It huddled against Eddie and worked its busy nose at his mother.

She rubbed his back through her bedclothes and nearly hugged him. But he sat still, not knowing where to look, and noticed how perfect and white his mother's feet were. They barely touched the floor and her toe-knuckles kinked white where she held to her balance. They were small feet, delicately veined in a blue very nearly the color of her remaining eye. They were wide, she'd told him, because she went barefoot as a girl.

"I brought this one so you could see him," Eddie said. "The whole litter is black-and-white, but this one is all black."

"Does he have a name?"

"No," Eddie said, "I thought you'd want to name him."

She started to reach out from under her sheet towards the rabbit, but pulled back.

"He won't bite," Eddie said. "He's the best one of the bunch."

When she moved, Eddie saw that one arm was much shorter than the other. One arm stopped just above the wrist, the other ended at the elbow. He couldn't stop staring at the dull lumps they formed against the inside of her sheet.

His mother said, "Put him here, on my lap. I can't . . . I can't hold him, so you'll have to watch out that he doesn't get away. They wouldn't care for a rabbit running the halls here, would they?"

Eddie picked up the rabbit and set it carefully in his mother's lap. He noticed that she winced a bit, and he realized how much of her was burned. Her back, where the gown fell open, looked as smooth and white as her feet, her backbone standing out like thick knuckles. She hurt her back at work just before he turned five and had to stay home and take medicines for a long time. They ate macaroni and cheese almost every night then, and Eddie would rub her back with smelly stuff every morning and night.

His mom would not take her arms out from the covers to pet the rabbit, but she sort of cuddled it there in her lap. She leaned one shoulder against Eddie and he kissed her beside her good eye. She would not show herself below her eyes, and forming some words seemed hard for her. He realized that she spoke in a whisper because that's all she had, not because she was afraid he'd be found.

Suddenly there was an elevator sound from the hallway, then dishes rattling in a cart.

"You'd better hide . . . oh, the window!"

Eddie hurried to the window and pulled it closed. He got up so fast he startled the rabbit and it scrambled off his mother's lap and under the bed. As the food cart banged the door open, Eddie slid himself under her bed, too. The rabbit was gone; he couldn't see it anywhere.

A pair of white shoes filled with white stockings walked around the cart and toed up to the next bed first, then his mother's.

Eddie's rabbit had left a scatter of pellets and he was glad it hadn't done that while it was in his mother's lap. Wads of dust-balls hung from the springs at the head of the bed. Eddie's nose tickled and he rubbed it hard so he wouldn't sneeze.

"Morning, Mrs. Reyes," an elderly voice said. "Jeanie will be up from therapy in a minute to help you out with this. My, you're doing so much better than Doris, here. We've got a full house and I've got to run. Is there something I can get you before Jeanie comes in?"

His mother cleared her throat, and in her hoarse whisper asked, "Would you open the window? I'd like some fresh air."

"I'll have to ask doctor about that," the voice replied. The shoes squeak-squeaked back to the cart. "Infection is the hobgoblin of burn patients. We don't want you to come this far just to lose you now, do we? Doctor will be in this morning, too. I hear that he has some news from that burn center in California. You be good for Jeanie, now, and I'll see you at lunch time."

The door slapped shut behind the cart and they were left with the wet snores of Doris across the curtain. Eddie scrambled out from under the bed.

"That was close," he said, but before he could say anything else his mother shushed him.

"Eddie, you've got to get something for me from home and bring it here right away. Can you get home and back in the window again?"

He nodded.

"Yes," he said, "but the rabbit is still . . . oh, there he goes!"

The little black thing crept out from under Doris' bed, testing the air with its quick nose. Eddie started after it and it darted away.

"Leave it," his mom whispered. "They'll be here in a minute. Go home to the bathroom and get my back medicine out of the cabinet. You know which bottle it is? Okay. If there's anyone in here, then wait outside the window until they're gone. Can you wait out there without anybody seeing you?"

"Yes," he said, "the bushes. . . ."

"Go now," she said, her voice louder, harder. "Don't stop to talk to anybody, don't tell grandma or grandpa. Hurry."

"But the rabbit. . . ."

"He won't go anywhere," she said. "Catch him when you come back. I need that medicine, Eddie. You have to do this for me. Now, go, they'll be here—"

Eddie heard the voices in the hall, and before he knew it he had raised the window, slipped outside and closed it. He waited a moment, listening to the therapist make small talk while she fed his mother. He sat under the window, knowing he should hurry on the errand for his mother, but unable to move because he wanted so much to see her face.

He looked once again down the alley to where it dead-ended into the lumber yard, and Eddie thought he saw the figure of a boy about his age scale the far fence and disappear.

The metal treads of the fire escape echoed his steps down no matter how careful he was. Going down the side of the building was scarier than going up, but he kept hold of the ivy and that helped. The last jump to the ground pitched him forward on his hands and knees. He scraped his palms in the gravel, and even though they bled from the scrapes he didn't cry.

He didn't short-cut through the feed store this time, but went the long way down the alley and around the lumber yard instead. There was something about the boy that Eddie had seen that made him hope he'd run into him.

In the years after his sixth birthday, Eddie would remember many details of this day. He would not remember the run home, nor how he managed to sneak past his grandparents. He did remember finding the big bottle of blue pills behind the cough medicine in his mother's cabinet, and he remembered the sting of the steel rung of the fire escape when he jumped up and grabbed it with his scraped-up hands.

This time, when he listened at the window, he heard hoarse barks of pain from his mother.

"That's it, Leda, we're just about done," the therapist said. "Let's try it one more time."

His ear was right next to the window now, and he could hear his mother's sobs and heavy breathing.

"No, please. Let me rest, *please.*"

"We need to keep you moving, Leda. If we don't keep at it, your arms will just lock up like they did at first. Aren't you doing much better now than when we first started? I think so. You couldn't move them at all, then. Now look at you. Once more, now."

Eddie pressed his head against the cool brick of the wall and tried to shut out the dry, empty screams of his mother's scorched throat.

He watched a trail of tiny red ants make their way from a branch of the ivy onto the brick, then into a crack in the mortar. When he looked closer, he saw that thousands of ants used the crack in the wall as a kind of superhighway, some of them stopping to touch antennae with each other in their two-lane scramble.

Everything was quiet in the room now except for his mother's heavy breathing. He peeked over the sill and saw that the curtain had been drawn around her bed and he could only see the lumps of her feet near the bottom rail. He raised the window again and stepped inside.

She was lying on her back with a sheet up to her waist. Her head was flung back on her pillow, and she gulped great breaths of air through the angry slash that had once been her mouth. She didn't really have a face. From the middle of what used to be her nose on down, it looked like somebody just pasted on skin, like the figures she'd helped him make out of newspaper and paste. She wasn't ugly, exactly, even though she didn't have lips anymore to cover her teeth. But he couldn't stop staring and he stood there, stock-still, until her breathing eased and she opened her eye.

"Oh, Eddie," she said, "I'm sorry . . . I didn't want you to see. . . ."

He left the window open and stood by her bedside with his hand on her shoulder. Presently, she lifted her arm under the sheet and touched his cheek. He knew he should say something, but he couldn't think of anything.

"Mom, I love you," he said, and kissed her forehead.

"Oh, Eddie, I love you too. This is such a mess."

He was going to let her rest some more, but she tried to sit up.

"Would you help me up?" she asked.

He reached behind to the smooth, warm skin of her back and helped her sit up. It wore her out again and she had to catch her breath.

Her breath didn't smell very good when she breathed hard in his face and he tried not to show it.

"I love you, Mom," he repeated. It was all he could think of to say.

She rested her forehead on his shoulder.

"I love you, too, Eddie. You have to remember that, because other people won't understand. But *you* know it, and I don't want you to forget . . . to forget me as I was, or to forget that I love you."

"I won't, Mom," he said.

She gathered herself up a little more and took a deep breath.

"Well," she said, "did you bring it?"

"Yes."

He took the medicine bottle out of his pocket and set it on the bed.

She held up her stumps and said, "I can't open it. You'll have to open it and get me some water. I can't use a straw yet, either."

He opened the big bottle of blue pills and set it on her tray beside the bed, and he poured a glass of water from her pitcher. The pitcher was big and heavy, and he slopped the water all over the tray. His mother didn't scold him. She didn't seem to notice. She took another deep breath.

"Okay, Eddie, I need to take them all. It's okay, because I'm supposed to take three a day and I haven't had any since I've been here, right? So I have to catch up."

"But Grandpa says that when you take medicine . . . ."

"Does it look like it can hurt me?" she snapped. Then she immediately softened her voice.

"It's my back," she said, "it hurts so much I can't think straight. Now we've got to get this done and get you back home before anybody comes back up here."

He helped her by giving her the pills a small handful at a time, each of which she swallowed with a big gulp of water. Eddie didn't realize until then just how useful lips were, because she couldn't really keep the water in very well. Her mouth on the inside was cracked and dry. What was left of her tongue was thick and smooth, all the little rough spots had been burned off.

When it was finished, she reclined back on her pillows, her arm linked in his.

"I'll get some sleep now," she said. "Thank you. You should run back home, now. Take the bottle with you."

"My rabbit . . ."

"Hurry and see if you can find him," she said.

Eddie found the rabbit behind the other woman's wastebasket in the corner of the room. It skittered away from him, and when he made a grab he got it by one back leg. He backed into the other woman's tray and it came crashing down on top of him, but he kept hold of the rabbit.

Footsteps came running down the hall and he ducked behind his mother's curtain. Her eye watched him, but she didn't say anything. He stuffed the rabbit under his jacket and clamped his elbow down to hold it. He snatched the empty pill bottle from the tray and stepped out the window just as the door to her room crashed open. He couldn't reach up to close the window and hold onto the rabbit, too, so he crept down the fire escape and hid in the ivy at the bottom until he was sure no one was looking.

When he jumped to the ground, the rabbit fell out from under his jacket and scrambled off into the weeds. Eddie looked back up at his mother's window, which was still open, then ran all the way to the trees by the river and didn't come home until dark. By then, his mother was dead and the whole town knew how it happened.

The Fight

WE call him Elvis because of the way he wears his hair and sideburns. His hair gives him a lot of trouble because he's Indian and it won't stand up in front by itself. Elvis got me the job working on the bulb digger with him. He said yesterday I'd have to fight for the job and from the new look of his nose this morning I believed him.

If it weren't for Elvis, I'd still be humping irrigation pipe in the berryfields for twenty-five bucks a day. But working the bulbs, on a digger, I get six bucks an hour and guaranteed overtime. Well, after this thing with Boss that's probably all washed up for us now.

Elvis came by to get me this morning at five. When I opened the door to his dad's pickup he said, "You got coffee? I only got enough for lunch." He's always been pushy like that.

I filled both our cups, which left me exactly one cup for lunch. I handed him his coffee.

"What's this white shit?"

"I like milk in my coffee."

"Jesus Christ on a crutch," he said, and sipped at it like it was rat poison. *"Jesus!"*

I was the one who smashed his nose down flat like that, back in sixth grade. Somebody else gave him that twist and the scar. He likes it now because he thinks it makes him look bad, and to look bad is Elvis's strongest personal goal.

We were the first ones to drive into that bulb field across the river. The rattletrap bulb-digger rested with its snout in the ground, glistening with sunrise and the dew. The long red monster hugged its furrow and its half-buried disc of saw-like teeth dripped away the last of the ground fog like drool.

Built as a potato-digger, it turned up the ground and laid it onto a chain-link conveyor that ran down its spine. Those giant saw-teeth rooted up tulip bulbs and rocks, dirt clods and rodents, then spread them out onto the chain for us to sort.

Elvis explained how the eight of us would line up and balance on those two flimsy running-boards. We were supposed to throw off rocks that jammed between links of the chain and let the dirt clods bounce themselves to bits by the jarring of the digger.

"Watch yourself," he warned me. "You'll get a dirt clod upside the head. It won't be the machine that does it."

The Boss showed up to start the engine and warm it up. Elvis introduced us, but the Boss only grunted.

Boss was older, between twenty-five and thirty. He got a bonus for every lug of bulbs we dug so he was interested in digging bulbs. He was missing a front tooth and entertained himself all day by spitting tobacco sludge through the gap at the stacks of boxes as he drove.

"The boys back at the shed bitch about it," Elvis said. "They have to handle the lugs. But none of them bitches to Boss."

As the rest of the crew straggled into the field, Elvis pointed out the beer coolers that Boss kept under his car.

"He sucks 'em down all day until he can't hold her on the row anymore," he said. "Then we quit. But he makes us clean up the digger first. We have to pull out every chunk of grass and dirt from in between all the chain links. He just gets off, says 'Clean-up,' then lays in the shade while we do it. Sometimes just laying there pulls him together and we have to work some more and then we have to clean the sonofabitch twice."

Elvis didn't have to tell me about the fights—I'd already heard. The digger works a sixteen-hour day, except for fights. When a fight starts, the digger shuts down and work doesn't start up again until the fight's over, because it's too dangerous. Somebody could roll underneath or get thrown into the teeth or the chain. Otherwise, the digger shuts down only for lunch, gas, or breakdowns. According to Elvis, Boss was a good company driver whose down time might not total

fifteen minutes in twelve hours. It was August, clear and hot in the
riverbottom.

Lunch was half an hour, barring fights. If there was a fight, then
lunch lasted until the fight was over. Elvis said that every fight at lunch
started at the very last minute except for the time Wayne put a snake in
Ray's lunch. Wayne was the catcher at the end of the digger who filled
the lugs with bulbs as they rolled down the chain. Ray beat up Mullins
for it, the usual mix-up, but it still meant twenty extra minutes in the
shade for the rest of the crew.

Boss vaulted into the driver's seat above the bright metal blade and
revved up the digger. The exhaust stack opened up right behind his
head, between his seat and the conveyor, and the racket was terrible. At
least we got to rotate around the chain, so only two of us had to work
next to the stack at a time, and only for an hour or so. I didn't see how
Boss could hear at all.

We all took our places on either side of the chain, facing each other
under the flapping canvas canopy in two rows of four. Dust from the
digger turned sweat to mud, and by the end of the first row our faces
looked like riverbeds with eyeballs and teeth.

The catcher loads those heavy lugs of bulbs and stacks them on the
run. Some crews have a gleaner who straggles behind with a lug in
hand to pick up the few stray bulbs that drop off the belt. That job
doesn't pay much, and usually goes to a kid who's a relative of somebody on the crew. We work without a gleaner, and some say that Boss
would be alive today if we didn't. That's hard to say.

There's one college kid who works the digger, his name's Jim, and
he's about a head taller than me. He isn't as old as Boss, but he's older
than the rest of us by a few years. Everybody in the valley knows I'm
already getting letters from colleges for football. It was inevitable that
the fight of the season would come down to the two of us.

I've had experience with this kind of inevitability before. My dad
was a fighter—Golden Gloves champion, Navy champion, then a professional for as long as he lived with us, which was about ten years.
During that ten years I fought as much as he did.

At school, the first week of first grade, we all stood one at a time to tell where we were from and what our fathers did. I made the mistake of telling the truth. Telling the truth has continued to be a problem in my life—people will tell you they can take it, but they can't. Fights have continued to be a problem, too, and the lesson started in first grade.

"A *fighter!*" teacher said, her thin face flushing, "My goodness!"

When I sat down, Albert Crow Dog leaned across the aisle and whispered, "You don't look so tough to me."

I kept quiet. Albert had been in first grade at least once before. I was always big for my age, but I remember he stood a head taller, even sitting at his desk. He leaned across again and said, "Let's find out how tough you are at recess."

Maybe it's genetic. I never had any fight lessons in spite of my dad's career and I never wanted any. But all I'd heard around the house was fight talk. I'd seen a lot of fights in the ring and out, and I'd met some of the greats at rent parties. After fights on Wednesdays and Fridays, they came over with their wives for spaghetti and pinochle. I learned that even winners get hurt, but nobody gets killed. The Kid Paret thing shocked even the adults.

Albert was a bully. He fought kids who gave up at the first punch, kids who thought a fight would kill them. I knew better. I knew at the worst it would only hurt for a couple of days. Albert didn't think it would hurt at all.

Albert was surprised, and that's what won that fight for me the first day of first grade. But the teacher whipped us both in front of the class until our piddly little squabble didn't matter anymore.

Fights are like potato chips, you can't have just one. In first grade, I had to fight Albert's older brother, his cousin and one of *his* friends, not always one at a time. This is my junior year, and I've pounded enough respect out of my classmates that they finally leave me alone. That includes the time Elvis pushed once, too hard and too close. He bitches, but he bitches at everybody and he makes sure he lays off when I'm not up to hearing it.

But I never really learned how *not* to fight, so when I see it coming I jump right in. Winning, to me, means just getting it over with.

So I knew it was my turn to fight on the digger when the dirt clods caught the back of my neck. It was only a question of who, when and where. I wear glasses, as you can see, and I had to step off the digger at least once in every row to clean them off. The dust caked on so fast and the sweat streaked them so bad that bulbs and rocks all looked the same. One weasely little guy, who everybody called "Rick the Dick," stepped off the running board with me.

"That college kid wants to fight you," he said.

I turned my shirttail inside out and tried to find a spot clean enough that it wouldn't just smear the lenses.

"Funny," I said, "he never said anything to me."

I jumped the running-board before Rick could say anything, and I tried for a glimpse of the college kid. He wasn't looking my way. It was a set-up, for sure. Rick probably threw the dirt clods and pretty soon he'd find a way to talk to the college kid and tell him how much I hated his looks. Or his sister, or *whatever.* Nothing new. I hate to fight when it's nothing personal.

One thing people don't understand. You can't avoid a fight like that, once it's in the works. You'd be backed into a corner eventually, with a crowd that may or may not be friendly. I learned that you could fight on your own terms and in your own time, or in somebody else's. Things usually turned out better for me if it was my time, my turf. I never set out to be a fighter. That's why I never beat up people like Rick the Dick, even if I thought they needed it.

The digger had one breakdown before lunch, but it didn't do us much good. Boss had spare links for the chain and he gassed up, all inside of five minutes. Even with the canopy over our heads, the sun and dust blasted us with cottonmouth and headaches. During the break, I saw Rick the Dick talking with Jim College, looking my way, smiling his weasel smile. Boss opened a new six-pack and fired up.

By lunchtime, Boss finished his half-case. We'd dug thirty-six rows, three rows to the beer. Boss snoozed through lunch. He'd stopped the digger in the middle of the field instead of working out the row to the river and some shade. We could always walk, except our legs were jelly from the chop of the machine, the fatigue and the heat. We all leaned against the digger and ate. Elvis and Ray traded sandwiches, Weasel and Wayne bitched about the sun because it was straight overhead and only threw a blade's edge of shade at the base of the machine. Nobody bitched at Boss for stopping us short of the river.

Just when our ears stopped aching, Boss fired up the digger. We jumped aboard in a swirl of blue smoke as the digger lurched along, devouring the ground. Boss hunched up over the snout, staring out to where the sun would set. Jim College lined up across the chain from me. Elvis worked to his left, and Rick the Dick was on my right. He pulled my shirttail and we stepped off the board.

"That college kid says he'll kick your ass after work," he said. "Says he doesn't like your looks."

"That all?"

"That's it," he said. "After work, in the trees over by where the cars are parked."

I jumped the running board again and looked for some sign of anything from the college kid that would tell me for sure it was his idea. We were into a bad part of the field for rocks and there were a lot of the little iris bulbs mixed in with the tulips. That meant we each had to box them separately because the catcher couldn't keep up. I caught an iris bulb behind my right ear. I knew it couldn't be Jim College, he was straight across, but the way he snapped a hard look at me, I knew he'd been hit, too.

So, there were *two* people trying to get this fight going. Rick the Dick had a partner. I scanned the crew on both sides. All faces but Jim's were intent on the chain. I decided that if I waited until after work, they'd all be ready and I didn't know how much Elvis would back me.

I handed my glasses to Rick the Dick and vaulted the chain. I hit Jim full in the chest with all of my weight. He tried to push me away but even though he was stronger and had the longer reach, I had surprise and physics going for me. He landed hard, with me on top, and I punched for his eyes because I wanted it over fast. If he couldn't see me, he couldn't hurt me.

The digger emptied for the fight and the air filled with curses and betting. I was feeling bad about it because I must have hit Jim College a dozen times before he even put up his hands. Then I made my mistake.

The shock had worn off, already his face was swelling pretty bad, but he protected himself enough to catch his breath. He never said anything, and neither did I. Maybe he knew we had no choice but a bad one.

Since he wasn't going down like I thought he would and since he didn't seem interested in quitting, I started working inside, just under his ribs. That was what he was waiting for. He made a wild grab for my neck when my hands were after his belly, and he got me. He had huge hands, and he got me good by the neck.

It was all over pretty fast. I thought he was going to kill me, because Elvis and Ray were trying to peel his fingers loose, while Rick the Dick was right down in both our faces hollering, "Don't kill him, Jim. Jesus Christ, Jim, don't *kill* him."

Then I quit trying to fight and just sucked any kind of air with everything I had until I felt all my skin tingle and go numb.

I must have been out only a few seconds, because Jim was just getting up on one knee and Elvis was slapping my face. Wayne hollered something about the digger. Everybody started running except for Jim and Elvis and me. Jim was bent over trying to catch his breath and so was I. Elvis rubbed my back. I looked up to see the digger wallow across the field at an off angle to all the rows. Elvis must have seen it at the same time. It was headed straight for the cars.

Elvis took off running, yelling, "Boss, goddammit, *Boss!*" but the digger plowed into the side of his dad's pickup and turned it over before it churned into the ground and stopped. Elvis climbed onto the digger and shut it off. The others stood in a knot about halfway across the field. Rick started running back towards us. Ray ran for his car.

"It's Boss!" Rick yelled, gasping, "he's dead. He fell into the digger and he's dead!"

Ray's car bounced across the field towards the highway. I helped Elvis back the digger away from his dad's truck. I'd walked past Boss's body without looking, but Jim stopped with the rest. Somebody vomited pretty loud, but I didn't look to see who. Pretty soon they all came to help us tip the pickup upright. Elvis tried the starter. It caught and ran, and he shut it off. Nobody had anything to say. The sheriff's siren and the higher whistles of the ambulance wailed from across the river.

"Go wash up," Elvis told me. "You and Jim both, go down to the river and wash up."

Jim's face looked pretty bad, and I had blood all over me from his nose. The sirens quit. One dust column followed the other from the highway. Elvis took my glasses from Rick and handed them to me. His hands were shaking.

"Was it you throwing dirt clods?" I asked him.

"Go clean up," he said, "you look like shit."

4

Eye of the Storm

Consider this a night on the mountain.
Words are stars, the only guide we know.
When weather's this bad we hole up, and sleep,
and count on a steady diet of wind.

Rocks under our backs press
into old dreams and bone. As we press back,
feel these waves that we raise around us
like heartbeats, arms or long nights alone.

Walking the Hills on the Cusp of Spring

for Aisling McCarron

First buttercup, bright burst of sun
between this starved cow's bones.

One vertebra, tilted up, fills
like a snifter with exquisite hail.

Solstice

This time of year, loons fill the night with laughs
and lovers bloom in beds across the dark.

A woman reaches out of sleep,
settles a slender hand on me.

There is hardly any night to pass.
One gray feather of dawn strokes her pillow.

Solstice morning, thick with loons,
the new air full with magnificent laughter.

Xmas

THE Jewish schoolteacher entered the coffee shop late on Christmas Eve and ordered a straight double espresso in a tall cup.

"You don't mind if my dog comes in, do you?" she asked the proprietor. "She's pretty old and it's terribly cold out there."

"Health inspector won't be by on Christmas Eve," he said, packing the fragrant coffee tight. "Bring her in."

The dog, a golden lab, shook snow from her coat, turned once in the corner and laid down with a *whuh*.

The woman, in her sixties, was a regular customer, one of the few who liked her espresso straight. She knew good coffee. But tonight the proprietor noticed she had some trouble getting her coat off, and she didn't perch the stool quite right.

He opened the valve and thick, black coffee dripped from a burst of steam into the white china. He nodded towards the paper cup that she brought in with her.

"Did you want that to go?"

"No, no," she said. "I need to be still a minute. Such a busy day. Are you going home?"

"No," he said, "I'll be here awhile."

He set the double espresso in front of her, no spoon. She never said much when she visited the shop, and she never took anything with her coffee. Tonight, however, she tilted her half-crumpled paper cup and poured something into her espresso.

"I've been to the grocery," she said, then raised her eyebrows as though that explained everything.

The proprietor caught a whiff of whiskey on the steam.

She sipped her drink and relaxed, still a little tilted on her stool.

"Yes, I've been to the grocery. And the butcher said, 'Come back here for a minute. Just for a minute.' Well, he took me back there in the shop and they were drinking whiskey."

"Wild Turkey, I'll bet," the proprietor said.

"Why, that's right. Wild Turkey. And it's very good, you know. But I remembered my dog was tied up outside and I had to go. But he gave me this cup. Full."

"Sounds like fun," he said.

He himself had already drunk two Canadian dark beers and was nursing a third in a mug under the counter.

"Do you have family coming for the holiday?" he asked.

She made a wry expression and sipped her drink.

"We have plans," she said. She waved a glove towards the window. "But this ice and snow—I don't think they'll make it. My daughter and my son. They have to drive from Seattle. How about you?"

"Same thing," he said. He ventured a sip from his mug, and the schoolteacher listened politely. "My sisters and their kids were coming, but I don't think they'll get through."

"We had our holiday last week, you know," she said. "And thank you for directing those people to my house. There aren't many Jews in this town and I thought it would be nice if we could all get together. So, we had our holiday. You know, I like coming here because it's always warm and clean and you can read here."

"Have you read that Hemingway story, 'A Clean, Well-lighted Place?'"

"Yes," she brightened further, "yes, I have. I was just thinking of that. I didn't understand that story when I was younger. You know, what's the big deal? But I understand it now."

"Yes," he sipped again, "I do, too. So, what brought you out on a night like this?"

"Well, I got a tree, a real Christmas tree, because my daughter's coming and I thought she'd like one. You know, she's a *modern* one. So I have the tree lying on the floor and I came down to find a stand for it, you know. But then I ran into the butcher and the grocery didn't have one and now I think I'd better just go home, you know?"

The proprietor knew her as a prim woman, very intelligent. Though the intelligence still shone through, some of the primness was melting under the heat of the Wild Turkey. The proprietor sometimes celebrated Christmas with his family, but usually not. Still, he had the right equipment in his closet at home.

The dog looked thirsty to him, so he cut the bottom out of a plastic jug, filled it with water and the dog lapped it up.

"Thank you," the woman said. "How did you know she was thirsty?"

"She's been eyeing our drinks," he said, and laughed.

He emptied his mug and went to the refrigerator for a refill. This time he poured it right out, seeing no need for discretion between them.

"I have a stand," he said. "This year someone was throwing away a tree and asked me to haul it off in my truck. It's a spruce, a nice one, in a pot. So I took it home and I'm using it for a tree. For the grandkids, you know, and my sisters. I'll put it in the ground on New Year's."

"Oh, yes," she said, "that's very nice. A live one. Very nice. Thank you for offering, but it's so icy outside, and once you get home you should stay there."

"It's no trouble," he said. "I'll mop up and bring it by. Can I get you another? It's on me, for the holidays."

"Oh, no," she said, "no, thank you. I've got to get home. Really, it was nice of you to offer, but don't feel bad if you can't bring it by. The ice is terrible tonight."

She shrugged into her coat, gathered up her leash and led the dog into the night.

The proprietor washed his dishes but closed up without mopping. If his sisters weren't coming, he'd have all day Christmas to clean up. His old truck started with the last spark of battery, and he drove home to pick up the Christmas tree stand and a cardboard box of ornaments that sat beside it.

He parked in the only spot of dry pavement outside the Jewish schoolteacher's house, left his warning flashers on, and rang the bell. All of the lights were on, including the porch light, but no one answered. He rang again, then peeked in the window. There she was, asleep on the couch, her coat for a pillow. She looked very happy and very warm.

The proprietor tipped his hat, left the stand and the extra box of ornaments beside the tree on her porch. He took out a brass dove, hooked it over a branch and drove home to finish the last of his beer before going to bed. He could not help but notice that her home, like his own, was a clean, well-lighted place.

The Tool

I CAN'T remember who dug up the tool. Four of us stood around our bonfire one winter afternoon, a full moon rising like the eye of God halfway between Christmas and New Year's. Blue afternoon sky pinked at the seams of evening, and the sweet bonfire smoke flattened out over the dark tops of hemlock and fir.

Four of us came to help Tom burn up his considerable slash before the state-wide burning ban took effect. Now, three days ahead of schedule, we kicked small branches into the fire and sipped at our end-of-the-chore beer.

I think it was Peter—short, blond, older than the rest of us—who kicked a hissing hunk of metal out of the fireside coals and batted the ashes off with a stick. He poked it towards Tom.

"I wonder what this thing was," Peter said. "If it's old enough, it could be worth something."

Judd laughed his eerie, nervous cackle.

"That's it, Tom," Judd said, pointing a shaky finger. "We've got to call the county, stop all progress. This here's a national historical site, for sure."

Judd was a tunnel rat in Vietnam. Now he's a claustrophobe who wires boats, and he was a little manic after a hard week in the engine room of some rich guy's yacht.

Peter took up Judd's theme.

"Yep," he sighed, "this here's now an archeological site. You've got to sift all the topsoil. Probably rare native plants, too."

The head of a homemade tool cooled from red to black at our feet. A huge U-shaped fence-staple was over-welded at the center of its arc to a steel cone that looked like the receptacle for a handle.

"Stop *everything*," Tom grumbled, and raked his fingers through his long, gray beard. "They'll sift the outhouse hole, too."

Tom always took things too seriously, and that was part of the fun of being with Tom. A half-dozen people lived in buses and yurts and a teepee on his property at the end of the road. This project would move the only visible bus further back into the trees. People out here value their privacy. Like Judd, many of them even set up booby-traps to keep the riff-raff out.

"Yeah," Judd said. "They'll get some Ph.D. candidate to sift the privy. Looking for the golden turd."

He poked another stick into the fire and winked at Peter. Judd loved giving Tom a bad time. He loved giving *anybody* a bad time, but most people just ignored him. Not Tom. The more Tom looked at that tool, the more glum he got.

"Maybe it was a fire-tool," I said. "You know, with a handle so you could stand by the fire and use that thing to rake coals together."

We all had sticks in our hands for poking and arranging the fire, and all of us looked at our sticks, and then at the tool. We all wanted to handle it, but when Peter put his boot down to test it you could smell the burnt rubber from his sole.

"I found some old bottles and stuff one time when I was digging post-holes for my chicken coop," Judd said. "I didn't tell anybody, because I didn't want the county poking around my place."

"Chickens!" Peter snorted. "Hey, I had a rooster once, Old Henry, a Rhode Island Red, and he was one tough sonofabitch."

Now, I'd had chickens most of my life, and worked for an egg farmer who had 75,000 white leghorns, so I knew something about chickens. I know that anybody who doesn't believe in aliens has never taken a close look at a chicken.

"That's why I was building the goddam pen," Judd said. "I had this rooster, half Arucana, half Rhodie, and he had this gold hackle that would be *perfect* for dry flies. I paid thirty dollars once for a piece of jungle cock hackle, and his was just as pretty. But he was so goddam *mean.* Like, when I was digging those postholes, he came at my back full-tilt and sunk both of those spurs right here where my shirt rode up in back. *Man,* was I pissed!"

Now, every rooster who ever tried that stunt with me was soup within the hour. Roosters are a dime a dozen, so I don't put up with that shit. But some people are a lot more patient than I am, and I didn't see the need to reveal the condition of my personal karma. I dragged a couple of the last big branches over and stuck the ends into the fire, then opened another beer. It was Judd's beer, and cheap, but it tasted good there in the crisp air beside the fire.

"Henry was a royal pain in the ass, too," Peter said. "But I cured the hell out of him one day. He used to come at me every time I came out to pick eggs, and about half the time he'd wait until my back was turned. One day, I'd had it. I'd just *had* it with that shit. So I picked up a two-by-four, and when he came at me I wound up and took a swing. It was a very satisfying swing. The appropriate part of that board connected with the appropriate part of Henry's skull, and he bounced off the chicken coop wall like a flat basketball."

"Chicken soup, eh?" Tom said, half-listening. His attention was still on the tool cooling at the fireside.

"Well, no," Peter said. "He flopped and twitched over there while I picked the eggs, and about the time I was done he'd got to his feet and shook himself a few times. But I tell you what, I must've hit his placid button, because Old Henry was a changed bird after that."

"Tuned him up?" Tom asked.

"Major," Peter said.

"Well," Judd said, "I fought that bird of mine for ten minutes. I punched at him and he spurred at me, and finally I got ahold of one of his legs. He like to beat me half blind with his wings, but I thumped that rooster right into the ground. I pounded that bird until he was nothing but bird jelly inside a sack of feathers. Then I threw that sonofabitch into my posthole and built the pen on top of him."

Everybody did some more fire-poking, and Peter picked up the tool.

"You didn't even save the hackle?" Peter asked, and turned the thing over in his hands.

"Nope. How could I go out there and enjoy a quiet day of fishing when the flies would just remind me of that ornery bastard?"

"Don't seem right," Peter said, "to waste good chicken *and* the hackle."

"Well, it's a cinch he didn't spur *your* ass," Judd said. "Here, let me see that thing."

Peter handed it over, saying, "Maybe it's a chicken-catching tool. You could just reach in and hook 'em by the leg."

I remembered how we caught hundreds of chickens for the fryer company by running low through the barns, fingers spread on both hands. Grabbing a leg between each pair of fingers, we snagged eight chickens at a time at a dime apiece and stuffed them into those little wooden shipping crates. We were chicken-shit and feathers from head to foot. My mother said it was good for the complexion, but she made me undress in the garage before I came in to shower.

"No, man," Judd said, "this ain't for catching chickens. Anybody can see that you use this on people who owe you money."

He held it so that the prongs faced upward, and gave a couple of suggestive jabs at a pair of imaginary balls.

"Shit," Tom said. "Put that thing down. It gives me the willies."

Judd handed it to Tom, and Tom turned it over, hefted it in his palm. He held it out for me to see, too.

"You're right," he told me. "A handle goes in here, and then maybe you use it to pry weeds out of the ground, or something. Like dandilions."

"I say leave 'em be," Peter said. "It's hopeless, anyway. You can't get rid of them. Besides, the kids like 'em. And they like to blow the puff-balls."

"I wish somebody wanted to blow *my* puff-ball," Judd said.

"Try taking a shower once in a while," Tom said. "That might work."

"Hey, man, those soap products are bad for you, man. Like putting fucking acid on your skin."

Judd didn't have water at his place, and after a day in the hold of some boat he didn't take to cramming himself into the shower stall at the boat haven. He tossed a couple more branches on the fire and opened another beer. "That stuff causes cancer, you'll see," he mumbled.

I scraped the fire off the end of my stick, took the tool from Tom and jammed the stick into the receptacle. Then I reached across the fire with it and raked loose coals back onto the pile. It worked perfectly for snagging small branches and piling them up. I handed it back to Tom, and he used it to push the fire together so that it burned a little hotter. That was good, because night was coming on and the crisp air turned to chill. He gave it over to Judd.

We all sipped our beers and watched the flames tickle the tool red as Judd held it out over the fire.

"Don't you all see what this is?" he asked no one. "It's the brand for Tom's spread here."

Judd took the tool from the fire and pressed it sideways into the block of wood that Peter rested his foot on. Smoke roiled up, and he pulled it away, leaving a scorched brand in the pale wood, a "U" lying on its side.

"There you have it, Tom," he announced. "The Lazy-U."

Then it was dark quick, as it gets in this country in the dead of winter, and Tom took the tool to poke around in the brush pile. He drug a branch around and, as he placed it into the fire, the head of the tool fell off into the coals.

Already dark was colder than we all wanted to be, so we stamped our feet for a few minutes, finished our beers, spit into the fire and made our excuses to head on home. As we stumbled the single-file trail to our trucks, Tom called out after us through the moonlit dark: "Hey, you guys! Nobody tell the county about this, okay?"

Judd cackled up ahead, but nobody answered, and nobody told.

The Golden Rule Grocery

ONE day the grocer came out to sweep the walk and saw the clouds raining blood in the streets. At first, he could not believe it was blood—he thought he was seeing things.

But why would I see that? he wondered.

Aloud, he muttered, "This is bad for business."

He silently thanked his wife for the green awnings that she had made him buy, shook his broom at the offending sky and hurried inside to talk with the butcher.

The butcher, a fastidious man, agreed.

"A little blood goes a long way," he said. "People don't like to touch it, you know, or smell it. That's why I wipe down each steak and chop and seal every package tight. My wife won't let me touch her unless I bleach my hands at night. Blood is truly a bad business."

Not a car drove the slippery streets, not a customer graced the door. The grocer would close the shop except then he would have to walk home and he did not want to walk alone in all that blood. For the fourth time, he rearranged his stubborn carrots, sprinkled his broccoli. The butcher put his chickens on sale and remopped the twice-mopped floor. Still, the blood rain fell.

"I hope it lets up," the grocer said, his eyes distant and his frown, genuine.

"Nothing lasts forever," the butcher replied.

"People don't think of food when there's blood in the streets."

"People always think of food," the butcher said.

"Not with the blood."

They talked of unhooking the long awning from the front of the building to stretch across the street, but even the butcher didn't want to wade in the blood to do it. They waved and shouted to the baker across the way, and to the watchmaker.

"What is this weather?" they asked, turning up their hands.

"Bloody awful," the watchmaker shouted back, and they all laughed a nervous laugh that frightened the grocer more than the blood.

Then, as suddenly as it started, the blood rain stopped. The butcher praised the Lord and raised the price of chicken, but the grocer hurried inside for his garden hose and his bleach. He hosed down the awnings, the sidewalk and the street as far as his hose could reach, disinfecting as he went. The sun baked the remaining blood to the sides of the buildings and to the streets. It dried quickly and flaked off, then rode away in a rusty cloud on a maverick wind, to rain itself on another town.

When the first stunned and blinking customer entered the shop, the grocer gave him a hug and a head of lettuce. He hugged each of his customers as they came in, men and women and children, and he gave each of them something to eat, something to sustain them and refresh them from their inhuman ordeal of isolation and bad blood.

5

Map of the Last Long Night

This way out of town.
Wrap your bag of clothes and your one torn photo
inside your coat. A black hiss of rain
darkens that glint of light up the road.

No cars, no scuffle of boots behind you.

This rumble around your eyes
this sudden crunch of morning up ahead
marks not so much the end of blister and stone
as the beginning.

The Road

New moon again. Tonight the dark
mimes lovers against a screen of stars.

Her particular sweat still on still air—
the rustle nearby is not her night breath.

It takes light to empty a bed.

Coming Home

One dark girl soaked and shining
on a mare in morning drizzle.

Double rainbow.

The Liberation of Father Free

FATHER Free pulled a wet Bud out of the ice tub and popped the cap. His cheeks were tired from squinting and the beer helped numb his perpetual tropical burn. It was a Saturday afternoon luau, three weeks before Christmas, and eighty-five degrees under the clear Hawaiian sky—a blue slightly deeper than his eyes. Father Free had come to realize that he would only burn and peel, never tan. His pink Russian nose was smeared with white lotion. A burst of foam from his beer made a tight swallow past his collar.

The annual St. Mary's Star of the Sea luau gathered around a firepit near the top of a grassy slope. From where he sat at the picnic table, Father Free watched Mokae Cove curve away like a great red boomerang to his right. The channel between Maui and the Big Island stretched away to his left. A smear of snow capped the top of Mauna Loa. He drank to snow.

Small black crabs swarmed the few black boulders poking up through the sand. Behind him, Father Free heard the bustle of the Hawaiian women closing up the leftovers in foil while several men tuned their guitars.

The men thumped out a rock tune, following a bluesy washtub bass. Soon they would play and sing Hawaiian songs until the crowd thinned out, or got tired of dancing, or until their fingers got too sore to play. Then they would sit around the picnic table, drink beer and play cards until there was no more beer or until there was a fight and then they would go home. But they could not go on with the luau while the priest stayed, this he knew. Several dancers were readying the signal for him to leave. This he also knew.

His neighbor, the young deaf woman Mai Kwan, was among those planning what he'd come to think of as "the haole priest's dance." They conferred beside the barbeque in a knot of bodies and laughter, pairing up and trying out the roles of goat, duck, snake and cat. They always did snake, though there were no snakes in Hawaii. Father Free had been here only a few months, but he knew that much. In every luau the snake always came out as some kind of comic penis spitting beer foam on spectators. He tried to be suitably discreet in his laughter.

Mai Kwan folded her beautiful arms and leaned between the Agoo brothers, her wide brown eyes flying after words. The afternoon sun flecked her long black hair with gold. This morning, and every morning this week, Father Free's dog had woken him with its barking. It barked at the bedroom window of Mai Kwan next door, who used her voice in love and who loved early these days.

Every morning, Frank Agoo's horse was tied to the breadfruit tree out back. Frank was married to Mai Kwan's cousin, Nina. Mai's quick brown gaze left the others, found Father Free. Then she blushed and smiled him a wide, perfect smile.

Father Free was thinking what a lot of difference there was between himself and these Hawaiians. He was thinking about it in terms of the affair that Mai Kwan was having with Frank Agoo. In spite of his priesthood, he didn't think of himself as a prude, as unreasonable. But these people at this luau fancied themselves good Catholics, good Christians, and most of them wore long pants or long skirts no matter what the weather. That was one difference between rural Hawaii and Waikiki beach. But the entire community approved of this reckless adultery—it was obvious by the blushes and smiles, the sparkling eyes lowered at just the right moment.

A bowl of potato chips clunked the table beside his elbow. The priest looked up to a woman's face unfeatured against the glare of the merciless sun.

"Eat something, Father," she said, "you didn't hardly eat. Don't you like Hawaiian food?" Nina Agoo's voice rolled up something in his stomach and set his heart-beat on high. Nina was thirty and her two keikis fought swordfights with sticks down on the beach. Now Mai Kwan leaned not so much between the Agoo brothers as into Frank.

His arm slipped casually around her shoulders and hers circled his waist. Father Free fumbled for a handful of chips.

"Thank you," he said. "There was a brunch at the ranch this morning. I ate too much there."

"Next time, I'll bring you some haole food, Father. You'll never get fat, if that's what worries you."

She sat on the bench beside him but with her back to the table so that the sun wouldn't shine in her eyes, or so she couldn't see the dancers, or both.

"You're like Frank, not the type for fat," she said. "He can eat and eat and drink all the beer he wants. He never gets fat. I probably put on a pound just carrying those chips."

She laughed an easy laugh and the breeze whipped her long black hair across her face. She pulled a few strands out of her mouth and shook her head to straighten it. He shifted on the picnic bench so that he could see her without fighting the sun.

Behind them, the guitars took up a familiar Hawaiian tune and three couples sang of princesses and warriors. Without turning around, he knew that four or five of the older women were dancing and showing the youngsters some hula steps. Father Free liked hula, which surprised him. It was true that all that was said was said with the hands. Maybe that's why he liked it.

"They are going to do 'Old MacDonald Had a Farm' again, aren't they?" he asked.

Nina hid her smile behind her hand. "Yes, they do it every time."

"If there are no haoles, do they do it then?"

She pursed her lips, thinking. "That's a good question, Father. I never noticed."

Turned as he was, sitting side-saddle on the bench, Father Free found himself following every move Mai Kwan made, every flutter of her expressive hands.

Another cold beer clunked the tabletop and Nina twisted off the cap for him. "Take a walk with me, Father," she said. "I need to talk to you about your dog and the fuss he's raising in the mornings."

The beer foamed up into the priest's nose. He coughed a little and recovered. "Of course," he said, his eyes watering, "the beach is perfect this time of day."

They walked in what people call silence but is actually the absence of talk and the intensification of little scratching sounds of wind shifting drying grains of sand, the irregular *thlap-slap* of waves against rock, and the fading chatter of the luau at their backs. A haole couple stood on a rocky point with their arms around each other's waists and their backs to the sea. Father Free turned to shout a warning just as a maverick wave broke over the couple and nearly washed them away. They met the danger with childlike giggles and shrieks, drenched, waving their empty bottles high.

"You can't save everybody, Father," Nina told him. "Some things they have to find out for themselves."

Nina slipped her hand into his.

"Don't worry," she said at his flinch, "I won't seduce you. You're the only man that a married woman in this town can walk with without people talking story. It's nice to be out here with you. People go crazy if they don't get touched a little bit, you know? Let's say that I'm trying to keep you from going crazy."

"Do you think that's what's happening, that I'm going crazy?"

She shook her head and her clean black hair hissed beside his shoulder. "You're leaving crazy," she said. "That's why you've started letting your dog out later every day."

He felt himself blush, but walked along without saying anything.

"There is a story about why the priest's dog barks," Nina said. She was not looking at him, but scanning the thick greenery above the beach. He watched the chop of the smaller waves against the rusty sand.

"It was four years ago," Nina said, "that Mai Kwan and I went night fishing along the shore between Pu'uiki and Koali. It was exactly four years ago. She was home for vacation from school and I wanted to get away from Frank and the keikis. Christmas was three days away—a woman gets a little crazy, Father, shut up all the time with two kids. So we went night fishing and I took the shotgun. Frank's always afraid of these dirt-baggers who come up the beach and the pakalolo farmers on the mountain."

A sweep of her hand indicated the bulk of Haleakala shadowing them from the right. He knew all too well about the marijuana farmers on the mountain. Confession, in a small community, had already become a terrible weight.

The sun tucked itself behind the mountain and afternoon shadows lengthened themselves into a pool of dusk at the water. Father Free had spent most of his short time on the island trying to accustom himself to the indirect ways of these Hawaiians. Indirect, oblique, gestural—he couldn't put a word to it. The waiting for Nina to pick up her story was punctuated by the small beach sounds, the occasional scream of a magpie or a child back at the luau.

"Let's sit here for a minute, Father. It's a nice spot to watch the water."

They sat on the corner of a low wall made up of smooth, round stones. Most of the stones on the top layer were wrapped in long, palm-like leaves. Father Free sat next to Nina and she picked up a smooth rock, wrapped a leaf around it and set it with the rest.

"Now we are in church, Father."

"In church?"

"Yes."

She watched the waves touch the shore without seeing them. Her focus was somewhere beyond the waves, somewhere in another plane or time.

"This is a heiau, Father. One of the Hawaiian altars. It is a holy place, very old."

Father Free touched the stones beside him and tried to imagine the old Hawaiian priests, the rustle of feather capes.

"Is it still used?"

"Yes, Father," she said. Her voice was soft but clear. "We are using it now."

The chill that rippled between Father Free's shoulder blades might have been the great finger rolling night down the mountainside. He knew, without question, that this talk had everything to do with Mai Kwan and Frank Agoo.

"So, Father. About your dog. It is good that you keep him inside later these days. That way he doesn't wake everybody up. Not everybody has to get up before daybreak to work the cows, like my Frank."

Was Nina laughing at his embarrassment? He couldn't tell. Even Father Free knew that Frank was a cowboy for the ranch. But Father Free had hoped that it was only he who knew that Frank slipped into Mai Kwan's cabin these mornings on his way to mend fences. Then Nina asked the question he was most afraid of.

"Do you know why your dog started barking in the mornings?"

He was glad it was getting dark down on the beach. She wouldn't be able to see the sudden blaze of color that bloomed at the top of his collar and ripened in his cheeks.

"Yes," his voice was a dry whisper back in his throat. He cleared it. "Yes," he said. "I believe so."

They both sighed.

"Well," she said, "Mai Kwan and I worked our way up the beach that time. She fished ahead of me and we signalled to each other with our lights when we moved. She fished, I netted lobsters on the rocks. The moon wasn't the best for fishing, I thought at the time, but she was getting away from school more than she was fishing. You know about the caves up there?"

"I heard about the haole guy who disturbed an old Hawaiian burial ground in one of the caves. . . ."

"He hauled eight bodies out of there in his wheelbarrow and dumped them over the cliff into the water," she said, and pointed. "Right there. Eight bodies, dried out and sitting up, just like the old ones left them. That cave is very near this very cave at Koali. It's true that each of these caves has a story. So-and-so hid there when Kamehameha stormed the island. So-and-so stayed five weeks there when the road washed out in a slide. This is now one of those stories."

Father Free offered his beer. She took it and, without drinking, handed it back.

"Many of the caves have supplies in them for fishermen," she said. "Food, sometimes matches and frying pan. This cave was a good one and had everything: a thick tatami for sleeping, a kerosene lamp, dry firewood. Mai came to it first. I got caught in a surge out on the rocks and it took me awhile to work my way back. My bag was full of lobsters and with the shotgun it was pretty heavy. I didn't see her light for a long time and thought she'd gone on past the point. When I got below the opening of the cave, something kept me from flashing my light up there. I saw a very faint glow. I heard a kind of a scream, and then another. Do you have a cigarette, Father?"

"No," he said. "No, I don't smoke."

"Good for you," she said. "I quit."

Her voice held a steely edge.

He listened as she breathed deep a couple of times. A troop of five keikis from the luau ran down the beach, but when they saw Father Free and Nina Agoo, they slowed to a walk, pretended to dawdle and then turned back.

"What happened at the cave?" He bit his lower lip to shut himself up.

"It was a dirt-bagger, all right," she said. "He was staying in the cave and stealing pot from some hippies up the mountain. What I saw from the edge of the cave was the top of his blond head and the top of Mai's white headscarf. He was on top of her. That close, I heard Mai Kwan crying. The kerosene lamp was lit inside the cave, down by their feet, and I saw what he was doing to her. He grabbed her scarf and slammed her head down on the rocks. A red scorpion was tattooed on the back of his hand. I was maybe ten feet away, and if he'd looked up from there I knew he'd see me. He held her down by the hair and had one of those big fishing spears jammed against her throat. It was already started, Father. I just wanted to stop him before . . . before he . . . you know what I mean, Father. I don't want to say it."

"Yes."

"So I laid my bag down and untangled the shotgun from the net. I crawled to the lip of the cave. When I stuck the barrel in it was only a few inches from his face, right above Mai Kwan's forehead where she couldn't see it. He saw me, Father. He frowned and I remember thinking he was still inside her. I didn't give him a warning, Father, I just pulled the trigger."

Nina's voice shook and her hand clutched her mouth. The gathering dark swallowed up her features.

"You killed him?"

"Yes."

"And Mai Kwan is deaf."

"Yes."

After breathing behind her hand for awhile, she wrapped her arms around her knees and put her head down.

"I nearly killed the both of us, too," she said. "These are lava caves. I got three in the top of my head. Mai got cut up around her legs. The lamp didn't get a scratch. . . ."

Father Free put his arm around Nina's shoulders and held her while she fought for breath and cried nearly silent sobs. Back up the beach the familiar chords of "Old MacDonald Had a Farm" started up around the fire. He was feeling more like a priest, now. Maybe it was the cool night air clearing the beer from his head. Maybe it was the woman's lost touch.

"Father . . ." Nina breathed slowly for control, "there were pieces of him all over her, all over the cave. He pinned her down there while he bled. She didn't hear the shot, just saw the flash as his head blew up. She had shot in both legs. That's what I did to her. The neighbors think I did the right thing but that doesn't make life better for her. She couldn't stand to have a man touch her after that. She was never with a man before that and she hasn't since. Do you see, Father, how this is? Why your dog has been barking in the mornings?"

"I see," he said. Father Free squirmed on the rock wall and cleared his throat. "Did you send Frank to Mai Kwan?"

"No."

It was blurted quickly, then:

"Jesus," she said. "Sorry, Father, but I sure wish I had a cigarette. But he's perfect for her, Father. Frank is a gentle man, very kind."

Nina stood up suddenly and brushed off her long, flowerful dress.

"It will last a month, Father," she said, "no more. It's true, there's some risk but here that's the way of things. Someone will say something to him one day, one of the men with a joke or talking story in a card game and it will stop. That is our way in these things."

Nina Agoo turned with a hand out to him and he let her help him to stand. He was a little unsteady from the beer and the afternoon sun. She led him out of the shadows, back to the luau. They walked in the shadow of dusk but her family, his parishoners, sat on the glowing hillside in the last light of an orchid sun. The dancers lined up, paired off, and the rest clapped or sang or played:

"Old MacDonald had a farm, eyai eyai O

And on this farm he had a cow, eyai eyai O . . ."

Delbert Kuu's wife, Lillian, danced into the circle to the whoops of the crowd, hunched over, making exaggerated milking motions at her huge breasts. Granma Kuu laughed her toothless laugh, tongue and gums babylike and coral pink. Behind Lillian, Delbert snorted, making deep pelvic strokes as he walked. He held his index fingers beside his head as horns and he lumbered about the crowd hooking his horns at the hems of the ladies' skirts.

Nina and Father Free reached the edge of dusk beside the firepit. Nina stopped him before he reached the others and held his arm.

"Father, I think you read more into this dance than you should. You hear confessions, that's your problem."

His attention was on Frank Agoo and Mai Kwan, ready to go on next. He knew what Nina meant. He wondered which of Old Mac-Donald's animals Mai Kwan chose.

"Yes, I hear confessions . . ."

"But these dances, they are what everybody already knows. The real secrets stay with you, Father, or they go untold."

As she spoke, people exaggerated their clapping to help Mai Kwan mark the time. They began the verse introducing Mai Kwan and Frank. Father Free knew what animal she would have to be.

In three quick steps he was beside Mai Kwan, laughing at the surprise on the Hawaiian faces and his own audacity. He took Mai Kwan's hand.

"You and me, ok?" he mouthed for her.

She nodded, also laughing.

"Dog," she barked in her bold voice, "bark-scratch."

"Puppies," he mouthed.

". . . had a dog, eyai eyai O . . ."

The two of them sillied it up scratching behind their ears, chasing each other around Frank Agoo.

". . . with a bark-bark here, a scratch-scratch there . . ."

He and Mai Kwan stumbled across the circle, laughing and forgetting to bark. They finished with a lick to each other's cheeks.

". . . and everywhere a bark-scratch,

Old MacDonald had a farm, eyai eyai Ooo."

Father Free hugged Mai Kwan and she kissed him a lingering kiss under his jaw. It was done.

"Father, you're so *funny*," she said, her big voice clear above the music. Someone in the flurry of back-slapping handed him another beer. Guitars whanged out the finish and everybody around them applauded, happy in their brown eyes and the last of the light.

6

Postcard to My Daughter from Discovery Bay

Night-rustle under the floorboards, scratchings of dreams,
or a pregnant cat hunting out quiet and dry dirt.

Outside, the lowest tide of the year frees the dead,
clicks its barnacle castanets and laps at the moon.

I drowse here to the soft sucking sounds
of clean dishes drying on the drainboard,

to this nervous patter at the cusp of my life
now making do without you.

Postcard to K

The ram skull on the woodshed whistles winter home.
A low rasp of wind tongues the yellowed bone dry.

My last night with you is that cocoon
dangling from a cobweb in its hollow eye.

The Single Man Looks at Winter

This is the month for dead things,
for sweet willow mulched to loam
and deer-stomachs dragged home
in the stark-legged shadows of dogs.

This month, whole handfuls of cocoons
rattle brittle and frozen in the eaves.
In this house, this month,
only the gray nails breathe.

Gestures

. . . form cannot be long sustained in the living.
                                        Loren Eiseley

When we touch, our skins sing the song
that seeds hum to mice each morning.
The burrows of your eyes
the warm hush of your breath
carry the only melody I know.

Out of all these trees
that ring their brittle minstrelsies:
Autumn.

Every year the willow first,
then alder. Smell that thick
placenta of their leaves.

Termites drop their tender wings
and wind hurries the nighthawks south.
Human beings, in ones and threes,
jacket themselves against the cousin rain.

Autumn. And its thin drizzle
molds all our stillnesses down to dirt,
to the tingle of new roots setting down.

In this gray town, come winter,
women glide from man to man
like fog between madronas.

Men pull on the beef stew smells of town
and hug their woolen lonelinesses tight against their skins.

That whisper of summer at dawn,
it speaks a ticking of seed pods
and rattles in the hoarse throat of morning.

Evenings we wander the damp tideline,
our vanishing point:
the eye of a bright and monstrous light.

Backcountry Spring

Daybreak melts the near-full moon to fog among the trees.
I step out of my modesty onto the front steps bare
to chill breezes fumbling through old secrets.

Such delicacy the morning has with hairs!

All the fat buds, these willow,
all the lush eyelashes of rhododendrons
wink at each other and nod as I pass.

Cold snaps a passing bite at my nipples.

Sunlight drops a hush so sudden it
stops my breath. Slowly the tiny eyes
of all my skin open, infantile and full.

The day withers and tingles in its small gustings
up my legs. My feet turn back to the house,
treasuring these clumps of grit they pick up on their way.

Five-Shot Poker

I WORKED in aerospace fixing jet engines during the war, and one night at work I bought a matched pair of duelling pistols.

"Trapper's pistols," Squirrel called them, but I never knew why.

Octagonal single-shot long-barrels, silver-plated, in a hardback, velvet-lined case. Purple velvet, with a box for shells. Fifty dollars for the pair. My pacifist girlfriend would kill me. Actually, she'd probably wait until I was asleep and then cement them into my boots.

Hooded sights—did I say hooded sights? And they broke down like an elephant gun to reload. Twenty-two long-rifle, very cheap to shoot. It's not worth having a gun if you can't afford to take it out and shoot it.

"They're worth four hundred, easy," Squirrel said. "You know that."

"Then why sell them to me for fifty?"

"The wife's pregnant," he said, looking away. "She's got me clearing out all kinds of stuff. I can keep my quick-draw gear because it still makes us money. But I'm selling the rest. I thought you might like these."

I worked two jobs and was in my last year of college, a criminology major. Squirrel had been West Coast quick-draw champion three years in a row, and he knew I carried a gun on my other job, security guard at a junior college construction site. The thirty-eight I carried for that job was a worthless piece of steel that I bought for twenty-five bucks from another guy at work. It really made my roommates nervous, and my girlfriend didn't know about it at all.

Dave, Gary and I rented a dilapidated house overlooking Commencement Bay. Actually, it overlooked the railroad tracks, then the lumber yard and restaurant, then the bay. And the second-hand place on the dock that had piranhas. Gary was an apprentice electrician, saving every penny to buy his own place. Dave and I worked nights and went to the university during the day.

Dave and Gary went to high school together. I went to a rival high school, and lined up against Dave more than once in football and in track. I knew him and liked him better than most of my teammates. He pumped gas and majored in Elizabethan Drama.

Our landlord was a Tacoma pharmacist who played pretty good jazz trumpet.

"Just don't make any improvements," the landlord said. "When it's gone, it's gone."

"What about paint?" Dave asked. "Can we clean it up a little?"

"Paint anything you want," he said, emptying his spit-valve. "No foundation, no roof, no nothing permanent."

We painted it black-and-white checkerboard, skewing the checks so that walking through the living room would make you tilt. The floor slanted from the kitchen through the living room and out the front door, which accentuated the visual effect. Gary complemented the disorientation theme with a Christmas tree, spray-painted black and hung upside-down from the living-room light. The checks worked great with the black light.

Already Dave and Gary were uneasy, knowing I came in three nights a week carrying a gun.

"I unload it before I even get in the car to come home," I explained. "I put the gun in my socks drawer and the shells in the top kitchen cupboard."

"I just worry about somebody getting wild at a party," Dave said. "I don't want anything to happen."

"Don't worry," I said, "I'll be careful."

"It's not you I'm worried about."

That night in the parking lot at work, I paid the Squirrel his fifty bucks, and he threw in two boxes of shells and a cleaning kit. I got off jet engine repair at midnight, then off my door-rattling job at seven A.M.

Sometimes I skipped classes on the days I pulled a double, so the house was empty when I woke up. Friday, noon, and an uncharacteristic sun turned Tacoma balmy in mid-February. Both roommates would be gone all day, so I could finish the fifteen case studies for my Probation/ Parole class.

I bought a case of beer instead and called in sick for the first time in two years. Of course, I had to get out those pistols. Then I had to check the action and the sights.

And then I had to shoot something.

I was sitting on the front porch at the time, dry-firing on the railroad-crossing "X" and the eye of the black cat on the lumber-yard sign. I didn't aim them at the restaurant or the second-hand store, or any cars driving along the waterfront. And I never loaded them.

That came after I swung around and sighted on the stovepipe plate on the kitchen wall at the far end of the house. The house sat against a blackberry bank, with a tool shed and clothesline between the embankment and the back kitchen wall. I loaded one of the pistols and shot out the locomotive cab on the stovepipe plate. With the other pistol, I got the locomotive headlight. I was aiming for the smokestack.

I crossed out those two holes with black felt pen and tried again. I was shakier this time, for some reason, so my right-hand shot just caught the edge of the plate. My left punched out the boiler in front of the cab. I was just marking out those two shots when Gary walked in the kitchen door with his tool belt over his shoulder and groceries in each hand.

"Thought you'd be in school," he said.

He set the bags down on the table and his tool belt over a chair.

Gary drank those wide-mouth green beers. He opened one, tilted it back and noticed the pistols. And the marker. And the locomotive stovepipe plate. He spit his beer back into the bottle.

"Jesus Christ!" Gary said. "Did you do that?"

"Yep," I said. "I did. I got these off a guy at work."

I handed him one, opened, pearl handle first.

"Jesus Christ!"

Gary hefted the pistol and took a long swallow of wide-mouth beer. He leaned over the table and inspected the locomotive. He stepped back, took another swallow.

"From where?" he asked.

"The porch. Sitting on the rail."

From the kitchen table we looked back through the living room, out the front door, past the broken front porch rail onto a horizon of sawdust dunes, logs and water. Huge saws shrieked through logs as thick as Buicks and green lumber slapped like thunder onto railroad cars below.

I handed Gary the other pistol.

"Can I try it?" he asked.

"Sure," I said, "I got two boxes of shells with them. And this case."

"Groovy," he said, and lit a cigarette. "Maybe we should put up a sign."

He nodded towards the kitchen door. From the front porch, I wouldn't have seen him come in until it was too late.

I tore open one of Gary's grocery bags and wrote out a note in black magic marker: "DANGER: DO NOT ENTER. Walk around to front porch." I hung the note eye-level on the kitchen entry door with some tape from the tool pouch, then locked the door. Gary was already getting comfortable on the front porch rail.

He aimed and dry-fired a few times, smoked his cigarette. We both opened another beer.

"The foreman and the other guys decided not to go back to work after lunch," Gary said. "Fridays the older guys sit out in their cars and pass around a couple of pints. About half the time they send everybody home."

"And the other half?"

"They make you drive up to Mooney's and drink with them. Of course, you have to cash your check. Then play a little pool, which I usually win, and a little poker, which I don't."

Gary chugged half his beer and eyeballed the crippled locomotive forty feet away. He picked a shell out of the box and loaded one pistol. He kept it pointed at the floor until he was ready. He aimed, then brought the muzzle down again.

"Poker," he said. "We could play poker. I've got that deck of cards the landlord left."

So we stapled the deck of cards to the kitchen wall. First, we shuffled them and then dealt them up there at random. We had to crowd them in close so that we could see all of them through the front doorway. Gary got to go first, so I gave him four more shells.

"From here I can't really tell the clubs from spades," he said. "The flushes are going to be a bitch."

He knicked the corner of the Jack of Hearts, reloaded and went high off the King of Hearts to catch the Deuce of Diamonds. He switched to the other pistol and got an Ace and Four of Clubs, then scored square dead-center on the Ace of Hearts.

"Pair of aces," I said, and marked off his hits.

"You don't get these if you hit them," Gary said. "They've been dealt and played."

I beat him with three kings. We were marking those off when we heard Dave scraping his shoes on the back porch mat. I let him in and he didn't even mention the sign.

He didn't notice the pistols or the cards on the wall. Dressed in his greasy gas station overalls with his name over the pocket, Dave just held out a piece of his mail and looked stunned. Its letterhead was the presidential seal and the signature was Lyndon Baines Johnson. Right at the beginning of spring semester, one year from his degree, and Dave was drafted.

"It's that Literary Criticism I had to drop and take over," Dave said. "It put me two credits short."

"They're supposed to reclassify you, first," Gary said. "Isn't that right?"

Dave handed over the reclassification letter from his draft board. The two letters had the same date.

"Shit, Dave," Gary said. "What're you going to do?"

Dave sat at the table, then looked up at the playing cards on the wall.

"Why are those cards stapled up to the wall?"

"We were playing poker," I said.

It didn't seem to register.

"My brother-in-law says I can join the Navy and get what I want," Dave said. "I'll have to be in a year longer than the army, but I'd get what I want."

This wasn't the time to tell Dave about my own brief Navy experience.

"What would you do?" I asked.

"I can type," Dave said. "Everybody needs typists."

Gary opened another beer for himself and one for Dave. He nodded at Dave's overalls.

"You've got mechanical experience," he said. "Maybe they'll put you in the engine room."

Dave shook his head.

"My brother-in-law said he'd tell them that I did his books."

Dave finally noticed the pistols when he set his beer down on the tabletop.

"What the heck . . . ?"

Then he turned around and saw the cards.

"Are you guys *crazy*?" He lit one of Gary's cigarettes, and laughed. "You guys *are* crazy."

"It's five-shot poker," Gary said. "Play what you're dealt. No raises, no calls, one dollar ante."

"Somebody's going to call the cops. *Jesus!* you guys are crazy."

"Nobody's called yet," I said. "And it's not really that loud."

"Yeah," Gary said. "I think most of the sound goes into the house, since that's where you're aiming."

"*Into* the house?" Dave stood up. "You mean you're standing outside in broad daylight, shooting into the *house?*"

"We're on the porch," I said. "No other houses can see us out there, don't worry. I got these from a guy at work for fifty bucks."

"Fifty bucks," Dave said, and chugged his beer. "They're hot for sure, for fifty bucks."

"This guy's honest," I said. "He's married and has kids."

"Hotter'n a pistol," Dave said, shaking his head.

Gary opened him another beer.

"If we're going to play poker, we'd better get to it," Gary said. "The mill's going to shut down here pretty soon. Dave?"

Gary handed him one of the pistols, and Dave couldn't help looking it over. They really were a pretty pair, hard not to handle with their chrome-plated bodies and black-steel barrels.

"How many shots do we have left?" Gary asked. "How many hands can we play?"

I did the math.

"Five hands apiece," I said. "We'll have eleven shells left over."

"Dave should shoot up a few," Gary said. "To warm up."

I hung the sign back up, locked up and carried an armload of beer out to the porch where Dave was loading a pistol and shaking his head.

"I don't believe this," he said.

"Those sights are right dead on from here," Gary said. "Pick out an ace, you can see your hit better."

He hit the Ace of Spades. He hit it again.

"It only counts once," Gary said.

Dave hit the Ace of Spades again.

"I'm warmed up," he said. "Let me get out of these."

He peeled off his overalls and hung them over the rail.

"Dave shot on the rifle team at school," Gary explained.

Dave uncrumpled a dollar bill from his jeans pocket and secured it under a box of shells.

"Ante up, gentlemen," he said.

We did, and I passed out five shells apiece.

Dave turned down another beer, so we knew he was serious and let him go first. He shot like a metronome, and knocked down four aces *bam bam bam bam*, just like that. His fifth drilled the King of Hearts right on the snoot.

The next hand he shot three kings and two queens. Then two queens and three jacks, and so on. I mustered three of a kind one more time. Dave won all five hands and never had to shoot for the straight flush.

Six shells left.

"Here," I said, and handed him five more. "Go ahead and do it."

"It'll cost you both another buck."

Dave felt so down over his draft notice that we would have gone along with anything that helped cheer him up. We anted up another buck apiece.

He drilled a royal flush in diamonds and collected his two bucks. The one shot left I put into an unscathed Three of Clubs. I got out the cleaning kit. If you get right to it, the rifling doesn't pit.

"Let's have a draft notice party," Gary said. "Let's just have a good goddam time tonight, Dave. What do you think?"

Dave took a deep breath and let it out in a rush.

"Yeah," he said. "Yeah, let's have a party. And steak dinner." He waved his stack of dollars at us. "I'll buy the steaks, you guys get the potatoes on."

Dave came back with three huge steaks and three bottles of Lancer's Red Wine because he liked the crockery bottles. After dinner it was getting dark, so we called around and put together Dave's draft notice party.

That night, the TV news announced that President Johnson had ordered B-52s to bomb North Vietnam. We didn't have a television, so we heard about it from Gary's brother, who brought a cadaver with him to make a point. Lee was a political science major who worked at a funeral home. His dead companion was a toothless white male on its way to the med school. A Doric Inn bath towel was tucked around its waist. We made Lee put the dead guy back in the car before anyone else got there.

I'd known about the bombing because I'd spent two weeks at work prepping the tankers and bombers, and putting together backup engine kits. We knew that something big was up, and guessed what it was, but we didn't know the actual strike date. I wouldn't have told anybody, anyway. I had to agree not to tell to get the job.

My girlfriend was really pissed by the time she got to the party.

"Is *that* why you couldn't see me all last week?" she asked me. "You were getting ready to incinerate innocent women and children?"

"I only work on commercial planes," I lied. I had to agree to lie to get the job.

"And what the hell is *that?*" she asked, when she saw the kitchen wall.

"Performance art," Gary said, then took his beer out to the living room and turned up his new Frankie Lane album.

"Yeah," Dave said, "it's a statement about games and guns. Party theme."

She ran her hand over the holes in the cards, lifted a Two of Hearts to see the hole in the wall underneath.

"You *shot* these cards *inside* your house, *inside* the city limits. . . ." She shook her long, dark hair, crossed her arms and looked Dave in the eye.

"Where's the gun?" she demanded.

"I don't own any gun, yet," Dave said, and took *his* beer into the living room.

"I won't stay in a house with a gun," she announced. "Where is it?"

As I reached into the top cupboard I thought, *She's an art major. She'll like this case and the mother-of-pearl grips.*

When I opened the case to show them to her, she slammed it shut with both hands, snatched it away and ran, full-tilt, through the black-light living room and out the front door. By the time I got to the porch, she was already on the other side of the tracks. I'd already had too much to drink to catch her, so I stood on the front steps with Dave and watched her climb the breakwater overlooking the lumber yard and the second-hand store.

"She's gonna throw them in, isn't she?"

"Looks that way," I said.

She never looked back. The first one she spun underhand like a sil-ver boomerang through the glare of the dock lights, over a sawdust dune and into the bay. A heartbeat later we heard the splash.

The second pistol slipped her grip and sailed straight through the front window of the second-hand store.

"Shit," I said.

"Shit," Dave said.

I chilled pretty deep, pretty fast. My unregistered gun through the store window. A kitchen wall full of bullet holes. A dead guy in the car out back. I looked back at the house and didn't know half of the people dancing in the living room.

I handed Dave my beer and scrambled down the path through the blackberries. I met Sally on the tracks. She cut me a wide berth and clutched the velvet case like a shield to her chest.

I was too scared to be mad.

"I have to get it out of the store," I said. "Will you stand lookout for me?"

"I will," Dave said, and huffed himself up onto the tracks between us. "Besides, I want to see the piranhas at night."

"Piranhas?" Sally asked.

"Two of them," Dave said. "Big ones. They're in a tank in the back of the second-hand store."

"Trapped in a tank . . . ?"

"I'm going down there now," I said. "Dave, if you want to play with your piranhas then pick up my pistol on the way out. I'll be lookout."

"I'm coming, too," Sally said.

They followed me to the second-hand store, which fronted on a gravel road that stopped at the breakwater. I used my jacket sleeve for a glove and picked the big shards of broken glass out of the window casing. When the hole was big enough I leaned inside, but didn't see the gun anywhere.

"Hey!" a voice boomed, "what're you-all doing there?"

Scared the living snot out of me, and when I pulled my head out of the window, there was Gary, laughing beside a very pale, wide-eyed Dave. Sally took my place at the window.

"Scare you?" Gary asked. "Dave's missing his own party, you know."

"I'll send you my laundry bill," I said, then nodded at the window. "The gun's inside."

"Shoot, boys," Gary said, and grinned. "This calls for an electrician."

He brandished a screwdriver from his back pocket and knelt at a box at the base of one of the street-lights. In a matter of seconds he had two screws out, a cover aside and the lights off at this end of the street.

"Now, I'll take care of the party, okay?" Gary said. "Besides, somebody's got to be on the outside if the cops come. You know, for bail."

"Right," I said. "Thanks, man, for dousing those lights."

"That reminds me," Gary said. He brought a penlight out of his other back pocket and handed it to Dave.

"If you get busted, don't ditch it," he said. "But don't tell them where you got it, either."

"They'll know you're our roommate."

"You're not even arrested yet and already you're ready to blab that I'm your roommate. The flashlight places me at the scene of the crime. Professional sabotage of utilities—they'll think I masterminded this whole . . ."

"Gary!" Dave said, and shined the light in Gary's face. "Thanks for the help. We can't hang around out here and chat."

We'd all had plenty of beer, and it was cold, there, on the water.

"You guys," Gary said, "you're too uptight to burgle."

He crunch-crunched away in the gravel. Dave shined the light on the window, and we saw that Sally was already inside.

"I've got to save at least one of those guns," I said, and crawled in after her. "Hand me the light."

It was too late. Dave was already inside, and when he flashed the light around, Sally saw the gun. She and I both underestimated my enthusiasm, so I was as surprised as she was that I dove past her and covered it like a Superbowl fumble.

"All right, all *right*," she said. "I'll talk to *you* later."

She fired some indignation at Dave and said, "Now, where are those piranhas?"

"You can't turn loose the piranhas," I said.

When I finished standing, we were nose-to-nose.

"Who's going to stop me?"

"They're tropical, fresh-water fish," Dave said. "This is salt water, out here, and about forty-five degrees."

Sally sniffed, but didn't back down.

"Then we'll just have to get them to some warm, fresh water."

"Like what?" I asked, "a *bathtub*? They're better off in here. Besides, these fish are *old*. . . ."

Dave was already on his way to the back room, with Sally on his heels. I stuck the pistol in the back of my pants, looked out the window to make sure we were clear and followed them to the fish tank.

"Sometimes we feed them goldfish," Dave was saying. It didn't seem the time to tell him that this wasn't the kind of line that would work on Sally.

"That's *terrible*," she said. "Why would you do something like that?"

"The piranhas like it," Dave said. "That's what they eat, goldfish. There isn't any piranha chow out there, yet."

"You two think I'm an idiot," Sally said. "I'm serious. Keeping them here in this tank is cruel. Feeding a live fish to these things is cruel."

"Beats dying belly-up in a bowl in the five-and-dime," Dave said. "Or in some toilet in Puyallup."

Dave had the light on the piranhas, so I couldn't see his face. But he sounded pretty worked up. And he had never fed a goldfish to these piranhas.

"It doesn't beat being free," Sally said.

"We can't turn them loose around here, anyway," I said. "What if they *did* survive? They'd wipe out the native fish."

"And small dogs and children," Dave added.

They swam to his light, these silver-dollar pancakes with teeth. They ogled the line where the light broke in water, where it shimmered in shadow like a thin, dark eel. They bristled and unbristled their fins. They were unsure, or not hungry.

Sally pressed a finger to the glass, but they didn't go for it. They never went for it, because everybody did it. Neighborhood kids dangled their fingers in the tank on a dare. Not a nibble. But they sure liked goldfish, and Mr. Myers let us bring our own goldfish or buy them from him for fifteen cents a piece. A tank full of hundreds of goldfish stood on the opposite side of the counter, out of view of the piranhas. A small mercy, and it kept people like our roommate, Gary, from slipping behind the counter and flipping a goldfish into the tank for free.

It never took long, if they were hungry. Usually, the piranhas would bristle, sometimes back up into one of the top corners, and quiver. The goldfish had two strategies: remain absolutely still, which meant sink, or flutter around like crazy. Either way, the strike was quick and all you really saw was a puff of gold scales and a few gold nuggets tossed around. The second piranha cleaned up the nuggets.

"We've got to get out of here," I said. "Dave, say good-bye to the fish. Sally, come on back to the house."

I had on my most mature, reassuring voice.

"Some things just have to run their course," Dave said.

I couldn't tell whether he was talking to me or to Sally.

"What do you mean?" Sally asked.

Dave flicked off the light. A night-light glow came off the fish-tank's heater and the piranhas flashed a couple of times, then held steady near the bottom.

"They're sleeping already," Dave said. He started whispering. "I mean, there's such a thing as *inertia*. Once you step out of a plane, you fall. Now, it may not be wise to step out of a plane, but when you do it's best to open your chute before you hit the ground. Follow all the proper steps to open it and you'll land safe."

"What does that have to do with the fish?" Sally asked.

"By being here as long as they have, they've built up an inertia. Getting them to the Amazon is the right thing to do. It's not the *easy* thing to do, and they don't know how to survive out there anymore, anyway. Anything short of the Amazon is just torment. Let these two die in peace, but keep people from importing more."

"Are you a philosophy major?"

"English."

"We could chat about this up at the house," I reminded them.

"No, we can't," Dave said. "There's a party up there. Music's loud, everybody's drunk. I don't want to go back there, just yet."

"The party's for you," I said. "People want to—"

"People want to get in my face about what I'm going to do with my life," Dave blurted. "I don't want to hear it. That draft notice booted me out of the airplane. Now I just want to get down as safe as I can. And get the GI bill so I won't have to work when I get back to school."

I heard someone stumbling behind the counter.

"Who's there?" I asked, and Dave flashed the light on Sally.

"It's just me," she said. "Go ahead, I was listening. I'm looking for a bucket."

"A *bucket*," I said. "Sally, come *on*. . . ."

"I'm not leaving here without those fish."

"You think I'm selling out, don't you?" Dave asked.

"Who are you asking?" I asked. "Me?"

"Everybody," Dave said. I heard him sit down against the counter. "To change the military, you need to get good people in it. I'll work on changing it while I'm in."

"We have buckets up at the house," I told Sally. "Help me get Dave up and I'll help you with the fish."

"You won't," she said. "Besides, you have your gun. I told you I won't be in the same house with a gun."

"It wasn't so bad," Dave said. "I won some money."

"I'll make a deal," I said. "Sally?"

"*What?*"

"Dave's right about the inertia. Let's leave the fish."

"But I. . . ."

"We leave the fish," I said, "and you can throw this other pistol in the bay."

"Whoa," Dave said, pulling himself to his feet. "I gotta see that."

"It's a deal," she said, and laughed. "Yeah, it's a deal."

Everybody made it through the window without getting cut, but Dave and I both stumbled at the same time on the curb in front of the pier. We walked out to the end and watched the diners watching us from the restaurant. One dweeb actually waved. Sally waved back, like an Olympic high-diver on the edge of her board.

"Hand it over," she said.

I did. I was glad it was too dark to get a good last look at it. She wound up and pitched it halfway to Seattle, and Dave whispered, "All *right!*"

"Happy?" I asked.

"Yes," she said, and raised her fists in the air. "One more gun-free house in America!"

Dave didn't mention the thirty-eight back at the house, and neither did I. Sally was happy and I wanted her to stay that way.

"Okay," Dave said, with a heavy sigh. "I can face it, now."

We made our way over the breakwater and back up the blackberry trail to the house. Gary had the bass turned up in his speakers and I could feel it in my chest as we got to the porch.

I felt something else, too. Sally's hand found mine as we walked up the steps, and she kissed me in the doorway. It was not the kiss that made me do what I did, although it could have pursuaded me to do almost anything.

"Stay here," I told her and Dave. "For just a minute."

I got the thirty-eight out of my socks drawer and the shells out of the kitchen.

"Here," I said, and handed them to Sally. "We might as well toss these, too."

"What *else* do you have in there? A bazooka?"

"No," I said, "that's it. Do you think you can pitch it in from here? That last one went this far."

Sally eyeballed the distance, then me.

"I want *you* to do it," she said. "Besides, you know that's what you want. You're just itching to toss that thing out there."

I had to admit, it seemed like the thing to do. I've never had a very good arm, but I did get it out past the end of the dock. Sally was right. I felt so much *lighter.*

I handed the box of shells to Dave.

"Well? What do you think?"

He hefted the box of cartridges once, twice in his palm. Then, with a tremendous *snap* he tossed it almost all the way to the restaurant, we barely heard the splash.

"Inertia," he whispered.

"Good name for a boat," Sally whispered back, winked, and nodded across the bay toward Canada.

Firebugs

IT was Mike's turn to drive the pumper, so I grabbed my air pack and got the regulator squared away in case I had to go inside. The call was a structure fire at Arcadia, and it was our third fire call to Arcadia in three weeks.

I picked up the microphone as Mike cleared the station doors.

"Six-Two-One responding. Structure fire. Cross streets Arcadia and Dennison."

The old Ford engine screamed and both radios blared broken instructions.

"Owner says . . . back of house off Dennison Road, he'll . . . at gate."

Mike and I didn't need to talk. We had fought dozens of fires together, so we knew that he'd position the truck and run the pump. I was nozzleman.

At midnight, after you've been asleep for an hour, getting set to fight a fire takes some adjustment, even if you've done it a time or two. I was glad to draw Mike for a partner, because I knew he could get me out if things got bad.

Arcadia was a large farmhouse only two minutes out from the station, and we were first on the scene. A side deck was fully involved, threatening the house itself. I got water on it within thirty seconds and the fire was out before the number-two pumper rolled up. Like the previous two fires at Arcadia, this one was arson, no question.

"What the hell is going on?" the owner yelled at the night. "Who's starting these chickenshit fires?"

From a bedroom window on the top floor, his eleven-year-old son peeked through the curtains. Mike noticed the kid, too. The only kid in the neighborhood who wasn't out watching the action. The other two fires, a tool shed and an abandoned chicken coop, could be watched best from that bedroom window. The back stairs led to that bedroom.

"Excuse me," I told the owner, "my partner and I need to check out the house. You know, just to be sure."

"Sure," he said, with a shrug, "you go right ahead. You guys are *great.*"

"Thanks," Mike said. He pointed out the chief who was turning the tankers around and sending them home. "You'd better talk to the big guy, there. He'll need to make a report."

I shucked my air pack, then Mike and I entered the house. The inside wall was a right-hand stairwell up to the bedrooms, and we knew this from our other two calls. We climbed the stairs slowly, putting our bare hands to the wall to check for fire inside, just in case. When we got to the boy's bedroom, he was sitting at his desk, reading an algebra book.

"Hi," I said. "My name's Bill, and this is my partner, Mike. What's your name?"

We already knew the kid's name was Ancil, and the kids at school called him "asshole," but this is how the book says you establish rapport.

"Ancil," he said.

He didn't close his algebra book, and he didn't look up.

"Look, Ancil," I said. "There seems to be a problem here."

"Oh yeah?" he asked, all pale and wide-eyed. "What problem?"

"We seem to have a fire problem here," I said.

Mike picked up a mug that said "Seattle Seahawks," then put it down.

"What kind of problem?" Ancil asked.

"An arson problem," Mike said. "You know what arson is, Ancil?"

We pretty much filled up Ancil's room, the two of us. Until you've had to fit into bunker gear, you have no idea how bulky it can be. And after a couple of hundred fires, it doesn't smell that great, either.

"No," Ancil said, still not looking up. "No, I don't know what that is."

"Well," I said, "it's a criminal offense. It's a fire that's not an accident."

"You know," Mike said. "A fire that somebody sets on purpose. That's arson."

Ancil didn't say anything.

Mike picked up a *Hot Rod* magazine, leafed through it, set it down. I gave Ancil the unrelenting hard stare.

"So, Ancil," I said. "About these fires."

"What about them?"

"Five years apiece," I said. "That's what the guy will get who set them. Five years apiece in prison. You know your math," I flicked the algebra book for emphasis, "that's fifteen years."

"Yeah," Mike said, "you ought to get out by the time you're twenty-six."

"What do you mean?" he said, and slammed the algebra book shut. Breath came fast over pale, dry lips. "I didn't start those fires."

"Yes, you did," I said. "And Mike's right, they could put you away for longer than you've been alive. But we've decided on something better."

For the first time, his gaze met mine, then flicked to Mike before coming back. The kid was starting to sweat.

"What?"

His voice cracked and he had to say it twice.

"What?"

"We took a vote," I told him. "All of the firefighters here voted, and we decided never to come back here. We're volunteers, you know, and we don't *have* to show up at any fires."

"But what if it was a big fire and the house burned down?"

"And killed everybody?" Mike asked. "Oh, that would be too bad. And I'd feel bad that we decided not to come. But the fact is, we're not coming here anymore. And you'd better watch your step."

"After all," I added, "this one would've reached your bedroom in another five minutes. And the stairs just inside that wall would be useless. You'd never make it."

"I didn't start those fires."

"Fine," I said. "Doesn't matter. We're not coming back, anyhow."

"Just thought you'd like to know," Mike said.

We both tipped our helmets back like the cool guys in the movies, and shuffled out of the kid's bedroom.

We rolled up our hose lines and refilled the pumper at the Dennison Road hydrant, then headed back to station.

"Think we scared that kid?" Mike asked.

"I hope so," I said. "I remember when it happened to me."

"What do you mean?"

"Well, I was in kindergarten when I stole the book of matches from my parents. Little Tim and I—there was another Tim in the neighborhood we called 'Big Tim'—Little Tim and I wanted to play cowboys and Indians. And you couldn't play cowboys and Indians without a campfire, right?"

"Guess not."

"We lived in this county housing on a gulch in Tacoma, so we made ourselves a campfire in the gulch. Except we knew it would be trouble if we were caught, so one of us had the bright idea to hide the campfire under a bush."

"I wonder which one?"

"Yeah. Anyway, you know what happened. The gulch was full of hazel-nut trees. It was August, nice and dry with some tall grass between the trees. The whole gulch went up like a rocket. Threatened about thirty homes. We tried stomping it out, but that was a joke. Must've been two dozen rigs on that call."

Mike reported us back at station to Dispatch, and backed the truck into the bay.

"So what happened?" he asked. He smiled a big, sideways smile.

"I got caught, of course," I said. "It was a mystery to me how they figured it out."

"Well, how *did* they?"

"Every kid in the neighborhood was there watching the fire. Hell, every kid in *five* neighborhoods was there. I was sitting on my bed reading a comic book. I don't know where Little Tim was."

"These two firemen came into my room. These were the biggest men I'd ever seen, with all of their gear on, and they were very, very unhappy. They told me I nearly killed every kid in the neighborhood, including my little sisters. They told me that my parents would have to get extra jobs to pay for all the hazel-nut trees and for all the firemen's wages while they fought that fire. They told me they'd never, ever come back to a fire in that neighborhood again and I could just burn to death for all they cared."

Mike and I stripped the hose off the bed and hung it to dry. We loaded new hose and coupled it up. Mike kept chuckling like he had something to say, but it took him awhile to get it out. Mike's like that.

"Well," Mike said, "my brother and I had a camp inside the hollow of a big old snag. Like you said, a camp isn't a camp without a campfire. I don't remember which one of us got the lighter, but the next thing we knew, the whole thing was blazing and it was pretty goddam *big*! We tried throwing dirt on it, but it was hopeless. By the time the fire department got there the fire had burned up about three acres of good hay and the snag fell on the barn and burned up the roof. A couple of the boys had a little talk with me and my brother."

"How did they know it was you?"

Mike laughed.

"How did *we* know it was *him*? How did *they* know it was *you*? We were the only ones hiding up at the house, trying to look busy. Man, they gave us what for. Nothing compared to what dad gave us, of course."

I hung my air pack up and peeled off my bunker gear.

"What do you think?" Mike asked, as he stepped out of his boots.

"What do you mean?"

"Should we send the little firebug an application now, or wait 'till he's eighteen?"

"We better wait and see if it's a cure, first," I said.

Mike hit the switch for the overhead doors.

"See you next time."

I don't know if it was a cure, but I do know that in my last five years with the department, we never got another call to Arcadia. The kid eventually got some kind of math scholarship back east. In the new firefighting basic manual they tell you to handle this a little differently, but whoever wrote that manual obviously never started a really good fire.

Bloody Marys and Chips

THE medic Harry Toledo leaned his lank frame against the back doorway of Mercy Hospital and took advantage of the evening breeze. The August heat had wicked sweat from him all day, but now he shivered with a chill that had nothing to do with weather and everything to do with death.

In three shifts Harry had not heard a kind word from his partner, B.J. She was a strong, quick-thinking Emergency Room nurse and, though she was eight years older, Harry thought her beautiful. She was also moody, her extremes aggravated by the constant stress of advanced life support.

The Advanced Life Support Team got all the nasty calls, and in the past three shifts they had jumped to a lot of nasty calls. He had just finished an hour of CPR, and though two people had died in their hands today, Harry had no complaints about their work. He had serious complaints about B.J.'s silence.

Her silence came from anger and he knew where the anger came from, but knowing it hadn't done much good. Harry had been dating a leggy young blonde, and three days ago the blonde brought him and B.J. a burger for lunch. At eighteen, she was six years younger than Harry.

"She's a baby," B.J. snapped. "Don't bring her around here. Watching it turns my stomach." Harry always respected B.J.'s advice. But this wasn't advice, it was an order, and it was personal, and Harry didn't like it.

B.J. came up beside him in the doorway and offered him a stick of gum.

"You know what happens when you give me gum," he joked, and folded the Juicy Fruit onto his tongue. "We wind up doing CPR ten minutes later."

B.J. just grunted, and leaned against the other side of the doorway. She chewed her gum and stared at the Olympic Mountains reddening from the sunset. B.J.'s eyes were still red and her cheeks a little wet from the last code. It had been a fourteen-year-old boy, a drowning. Before the hour in the ER, they had worked for a half-hour in the back of the ambulance careening around Discovery Bay at seventy miles an hour.

Harry's memories of the afternoon included the boy's blue lips and half-open blue eyes, his regurgitated peanut butter sandwich that jammed up his airway and made him impossible to intubate. Harry had a firefighter holding his belt while he did chest compressions. B.J. knelt behind him and pulled the boy's arm between Harry's legs to start the IV. All Harry could see was her hand, the needle and the dim noodle of a vein.

"Tell me when you're ready," he said. "I'll hold the downstroke to give you some pressure."

B.J. leaned her forehead against his butt and, while the ambulance rocked and rolled, whispered to herself, "I have everything I need . . . right . . . here." And she was in.

"Shit, Babe, that was beautiful."

"Don't call me 'Babe.'"

She taped up the IV and started pushing drugs.

Sweat had dripped from Harry to the boy's pale chest during CPR, and when it was over, neither he nor B.J. could remember his name. The hospital had sent Harry to a workshop once that told him that forgetting names of the dead was normal, a survival trait that medics shared with combat vets.

B.J. interrupted his reverie.

"Not every time," she said. "Just once."

"Just once? Just once, what?"

"I only gave you gum once, the first time I ever rode in the ambulance. That cardiac arrest in the condos out at the point."

Harry was glad she finally felt like talking.

"Yeah," he said, "you really got a load of it that day. I felt bad, because there was no way I could convince you that it wasn't always like that."

"I wanted to quit right there and stick to the hospital."

"You didn't. And now you know."

"Yeah. Now I know."

Harry was encouraged. This was the best they'd done in days and he didn't want to press it. She had been a nurse before Harry had finished high-school, but taking nurses to the scene was a new experiment for the Emergency Room. As senior medic, Harry had to show her the ropes.

Usually, after a call like the last one, they would've been hugging by now. Harry stayed on his side of the doorway.

The breeze and the chatter of floor nurses in the hallway behind them lulled the frantic edges of Harry's nerves. He whiffed popcorn on the air and remembered that he hadn't eaten all day. The charge nurse on second shift always made popcorn, and she'd be down in a minute to invite them up to the nurses' station to share it and to review the codes.

Harry really didn't want to talk about it. There was no way they could've saved that kid, but the code wasn't wasted. In Harry's mind, the drowning was her final exam and B.J. passed even though the patient died.

The smell of the popcorn and the taste of the gum reminded him of the first day that B.J. rode the ambulance. Two months ago almost to the day, just after B.J. split up with her husband—Harry remembered it as the day of bloody marys and chips.

They'd cleared out a dozen patients in an hour and were taking a breather when she offered him the gum. Immediately, the tones from their radio started them scrambling.

"Man down, 22 Loop Drive at the point," dispatch said. "Calling party hung up. Med 18 en route. Time out, 1733."

"Man down" was the kind of call that Harry hated most. The man could be tired, drunk or dead. One out of ten times, it was a real mess. Harry grabbed the backpack with the code drugs and B.J. snatched up the defibrillator. They met Med 18 at the back door, threw their gear inside and strapped in.

Harry started a check-list.

"If it's a code, we want to stay out of each other's way. You intubate and I'll set up the monitor. If he's v-fib, I'll shock him right away. If not, whoever's free first starts the IV. We'll run the whole thing right there unless we have a problem."

"Who's doing CPR?"

Harry nodded towards the front of the ambulance, where Tom was driving and Randy handled the radio.

"They will," he said. "We'll take over on the way in. But be flexible, anything can happen."

Randy hollered at them over the wail of the siren, "Dispatch says we have CPR in progress. ETA three minutes."

"What now?" B.J. asked.

"I'll get an IV set," Harry said. "Pick out your blade and get ready to intubate. These guys can grab the drugs. I'll get the defibrillator."

By the time Harry had the IV primed, the ambulance slid into the parking lot of the condo complex. They lugged their gear in a dead run through the inevitable crowd outside and down the narrow hallway. Harry set the defibrillator beside the dead guy's shoulder. He couldn't avoid the huge pool of red vomit. A firefighter was doing chest compressions, but no one was doing mouth-to-mouth.

B.J. knelt at the guy's head and tilted his chin back to clear the airway. When she did that, he puked again all over her white pants. Bright red puke.

"Jesus!" she said.

She was already sweating so hard that her glasses slid way down her nose.

A tipsy woman who turned out to be the wife said, "He's been drinking bloody marys all day and eating those chips, and he knew better. The doctor told him not to do that. He had chest pain all day yesterday but he wouldn't let me call anybody because the kids are coming up. . . ."

Harry tuned her out and concentrated on ripping off the fouled shirt and attaching the leads. The guy's skin was cold and damp, and he was mottled purple. He'd been in big trouble for awhile; it didn't look good.

No matter how often Harry did this, he recited the same ritual to himself as he pasted the contacts onto the patient: *White to right, red to ribs, green left over.* He flipped the monitor switch and greased his paddles, just in case. The monitor showed a thin, nervous line over the lumps of CPR.

"Looks like very fine v-fib," he said, "stand clear."

B.J. was struggling with the tube, and just then it slid in.

"Wait," she said, "check for breath sounds."

Harry flipped his stethoscope on and placed the bell on the dead guy's chest while B.J. blew through the tube. He didn't hear anything in either lung.

"No. You must be in his stomach."

Then the guy vomited again, and B.J. caught a huge mouthful through the tube. She jumped so suddenly that she lost her glasses and gagged as she spit out the mess.

"I've got to shock," Harry said, "stand clear."

He placed the paddles, triggered the switch and nothing happened. He triggered the switch again. Nothing.

"Do it!" B.J. snapped.

"I did," he said. "Battery's dead."

Harry flipped the battery out of the paddle side and replaced it with the battery from the monitor side.

"Stand clear," he said again, and everybody backed off.

Harry delivered a shock and the guy jumped like he'd been kicked. Harry switched the battery back to check the monitor. No change. He made the switch again, cleared again, shocked again, and switched the battery back to the monitor. It was very faint, and there was no change.

"CPR," he ordered. "Any luck with that tube?"

"I can't see his vocal cords," B.J. said. "He's jammed full with crud. . . ."

"Then bag him," Harry said. "It's better than nothing."

The monitor was too faint to read.

"Batteries are gone," Harry said. "Let's roll."

The hallway was too narrow for CPR, so they hurried him to the porch, and it was there that Harry decided to pump in a couple of quick breaths. He felt a clear airway, but he'd forgotten about his gum, which shot into the guy's lungs with his first breath. Harry finger-swept the patient's mouth but couldn't find it, so he pumped in another breath and this time it was his turn to catch a mouthful.

In the ambulance they started IVs, gave the right drugs, kept up CPR. When they intubated successfully in the ER, out popped the wad of gum. B.J. caught his gaze and her brown eyes widened, but she didn't say anything.

"I'll bet he aspirated his gum and that's what started it," the doc said.

"Chest pain for two days," Harry mumbled, and concentrated on compressions. "Not likely."

The patient was pronounced quickly, and lab results confirmed that he'd been unsalvageable. In their two months together since that call Harry and B.J. became the best code team in the county. Harry was proud of their record, in spite of how today's drowning had turned out.

"Popcorn's on," the charge nurse called.

At the nurses' station, Harry filled their bowls and handed one to B.J. She smiled and nodded her thanks. One of the floor nurses said, "It's a shame you two had to lose that boy. . . ."

Someone shushed her. In the awkward silence that followed, B.J. munched a handful of popcorn and said, "Harry, we've talked for months about having a drink together after work and we've never done it. How about tonight?"

Harry felt a strange hysteria bubble up that he didn't know how to handle. Before he could get control, he heard his mouth say, "You don't remember?"

"Remember what?" she asked.

She looked beautiful in spite of the sweat, and genuinely concerned, her hand halfway between her popcorn and her mouth. An unpopped kernel nestled in the corner of her lip.

"Our date, two months ago."

B.J.'s brow furrowed, and all of the nurses who had been crunching their popcorn suddenly fell silent. An uncharacteristic blush washed her cheeks.

"I'm sorry, Harry, I don't remember. . . ."

The hysteria bubble that Harry held back burst out in a rush.

"Two months ago, B.J. How could you forget? You had me out to the point one day for bloody marys and chips."

She dropped her popcorn bowl on the desk and grabbed him in a tight bear hug.

"You're such a cold bastard," she whispered against his neck.

Then Harry hugged her back, lifting her off the floor before he set her down again. They both started to laugh, and the floor nurses sat staring at them in awkward silence.

"You're such a cold bastard, Harry," she whispered, "but *god* I love working with you."

7

Food Chain

Eisenhower shot Eddie Slovik for stealing bread,
for not killing Germans. After the forty days,
Christ ate what he could—stale bread, vinegar.
Gandhi stopped eating so his people would not kill.

Somewhere a pride of hungry shadows scrapes stone, shifts weight.
Every border, every fence, bulkhead and screen, every curtain
strains to wall out hunger, wall in fine fat babies.
More ingenious than fruit, we fall any season.

Gandhi died with soup in his bowl, shot for rice,
his dead mouth gulping down the free sour wind.
We are the only netted fish who pull our own nets.
We are the only game we harvest we refuse to eat.

Glimpse of the Death Squad

Guatemala, 1983

The Maya woman in the bright red collar
sells melon slices in the doorway shade.
She flicks flies from the lips of her daughter
curled on the rag at our feet.

Two men in gray suits lean in the sun
against the open doors of their brown Ford Bronco.
Their mirror sunglasses reflect four northamericans
glancing up from four tiny Maya women.

The warm watermelon drips on the blanket.
I hold it away from my shirt, step to the curb
and both men stiffen. One unbuttons his jacket,
reaches inside smooth as a magician, a gambler.

On the front seat: a clipboard, a walkie-talkie,
and a new Uzi submachine gun, folded like a bud.
On the clipboard: three names, too small to read.
The four tiny Americans take four red bites of melon.

We smile at the driver, toast him with the rind.
He nods. Those Maya women in his sunglasses
never look up. The windows in the Bronco are black.
I've never tasted a fruit so juicy, so sweet.

Petén 1983

*What can you do when you have hunger all the time and
the bugs don't let you sleep?*

guatemalteca

Soldiers disperse for the night in their grim
tight patrols. The Maya woman tending bar
smiles them a thin-lipped smile. "They don't please me,"
she whispers. "They don't please me."

They potshoot monkeys in the bush, save the rum
for themselves. They quit shooting buzzards
when the dead just stank longer.
A stutter of unsteady fire signals last call.

Listen here to the warble of night-toads
down by the lake. Smell the sweet bloom
of white nuns lining the roadside.
Like us, this country was made for love.

Where the Word for Wait is Hope

Sunset bloodies every face it touches.
Lovers stroll their secrets, soldiers
roll their tongues across unkissed lips
and stroke their short automatics.

Weight shifts, shadows pool in the street,
safeties click to the rhythm of a daydream,
to the sway of tight northamerican jeans.
A blind drummer chainsmokes Winstons at the bar.

From alley-mouths come the sucking sounds
of time at the breast, of dark history
swallowing somebody whole. Bloody snouts
root barbed wire and glass.

Love survives in soft tongues and whispers.
Life depends on signs: two rocks pinning a red bandana,
a branch across the road, the right word.
Geography here reflects politics and the wind.

That one-armed lottery vendor's fingers
fold and re-fold somebody's chances.
Tonight jaguars and monkeys run the streets,
the moon itself a million-caliber scar.

Learning the Ropes

You ask me how it started. Well, it was just a phone call to ask Miguelito to dinner. A simple thing, I know, but this was only my second trip as a correspondent so I didn't think twice about calling from my hotel. Then, when the desk clerk offered to put the call through for me, I was relieved. My Spanish is clumsy even now, as you can tell, and it is most clumsy on the telephone.

Yes, the clerk put through the call and I made the date with Miguelito for dinner. When he became a half hour late, I opened the wine—you know how difficult it is to get good wine in this country. After the hour, I ordered shrimps, little pink tongues licking at a scoop of hot rice.

Miguelito liked the ladies, it's true. He was a lieutenant in your country's special forces, you must have known that. He said he was fed up with killing Indians in the highlands.

"No more newspapers," he'd told me last time, "no more television. I only want my stereo, sometimes brandy, a little job that's no trouble. . . ." He apologized for what he said about the newspapers— he had sensitivity about my feelings.

"You are a journalist," he said, "and it is your job. But like the army, the police, you must get depressed, no? All that garbage."

You see, he had sensitivity for the police, too. That was months ago, after the first coup. He was just twenty-two that day, and we rode the lakeside in his black Chevy pickup. His tapedeck blared "Sympathy for the Devil" to the parrots and the sad, skinny pigs.

We stopped at a stone hut for the only cold beer I have found in this country. They gave us sausage piled on tiny tortillas that your people call "mouths." The beer was Rooster beer, so cold it gave us both that quick headache—you know it? The *pat-pat-pat* of tortillas between palms, the scratch of brooms in the street, the clunks of our bottles on the table . . . altitude ripened the alcohol in our lips and fingertips. He told me the stories of the villages that day.

"We built them a community laundry," he said. "We made it so that they could have hot and cold water, but in facing rows of tubs, so the women could visit like they did at the river. We built them a toilet and had to show them how to use it. They thought it was for washing their faces."

He laughed with his mouth, then, showing off his fine teeth.

But his sad eyes did not change.

"After the coup we came back," he told me. "They remembered us, and everyone came to the square wondering what we who brought them toilets and hot water brought them now."

He tried a swallow of beer, but his throat must have been too tight and he spit it back into the bottle, shaking his head. He went on, his voice hushed, and asked me, "You have heard the government's story, about how the village was overrun by subversives dressed in army uniforms?"

I nodded.

He brushed his fingertips across his eyes and a pale lizard crawled the wall beside us.

"It was us," he said. "We killed them. Every one."

He sighed, averted his eyes, and the hand that held the beer trembled. He leaned back against the stone, facing away from me, and I sat still. He cleared his throat, but his voice shook like his hand.

"I will take you there," he said. "If you write this, people will die. If you don't, then more will die and this killing will never stop."

Of course I asked him, "What about you? This is a small country. If I write this, won't they come for you?"

He wiped his eyes and blew his nose on a bandana from his back pocket.

"When you live here awhile, you learn the ropes," he said. "There were fifty-two of us. We are not invisible, like the Indians."

A few days later, after I had the pictures and the story, he drove me to the airport. He hugged me like a brother.

"Come back," he said. "Come back so we can celebrate the beginning of the end of the killing."

So I came back, as you know. I made that call, and he didn't show up for dinner. I finished the last of the wine and then stood to see what started a commotion at the dining room doorway. A journalist is paid to be curious.

The doorman and two waiters were holding people back. In the center of the circle of the tips of their shoes lay Miguelito's head, staining the steps. A wadded-up page of newsprint was stuffed between his teeth. Wrapped inside lay his tongue, pale curl of blue-veined tongue.

They have taken him away now. Maybe the others can tell you more. This is how Miguelito retired. This is how we celebrate the beginning of the end of the killing.

Where Hope Means Pray Here and Die

THIS is Sunday, and the Pope is still in El Salvador. Here in Guatemala, the people try to prove that they and only they know how to welcome a Pope. The President of Guatemala, General Rios Montt, is an evangelist preacher at The Church of the Word of California. The structure itself is topped by two fifty-caliber machine guns and it sits behind the National Palace. General Montt sees to it that even his country's protestants hang out banners of greeting for his fellow Man of God. There is only guarded talk of the six executions earlier in the week, inside the complex that includes the Church of the Word.

It is a sunny morning in Centroamerica Park, and the air is thick with fine spring blooms. Today, no vehicles clog the streets or the atmosphere of Guatemala City. So many pilgrims choke the roads that buses and cars park at the outskirts of town. Everyone is on foot, including almost two million visitors. Hundreds of thousands walked from Mexico, from the jungles of Petén. These faithful, "catechistas," transcended hunger, bloody feet and fatigue, and they make the patrols of soldiers and cattle cars of police invisible by wishing them so.

Here, beside the park, the people drag a three-story plywood cross from the back of a flatbed truck and lay it out in the street. The army watches nervously because this is a crowd and it is at the intersection of the Cathedral and the National Palace. The gathering crowd spills out of the intersection onto a green carpet of pine needles being laid out as a path for the Pope. I buy a Guatemalan hot dog and straggle along the fringes, speaking with a corps of volunteer firemen. I trained another group a few months ago, and I'm the first northamerican fireman they've met. As an emergency medical technician, I receive a great deal of deference. Indeed, fewer people are so trained in their entire nation than we have in eastern Jefferson County alone.

As we trade our firefighter stories, I sling my jacket over my shoulder. Inside the pockets are my passport and plane ticket out. Also inside is my all-purpose, lightweight first-aid kit—a few packets of sterile gauze and a roll of Kling.

A motorcycle shoots out of a side street behind the crowd, and the driver tries to slow down for the intersection. The bike slips on the carpet of pine needles and goes down, spinning on its side. The driver and his passenger, a young woman, are both wearing helmets but the girl goes down underneath the bike.

Her pain and fear make it difficult for her to talk, and none of the firefighters present move to help her. They indicate that all ambulances are at the airport and the Pope's destination, and, besides, we would all grow old waiting for them to fight their way through the miles of milling people. The firefighters handle the crowd, very nervously eyeing the army patrols working our way from the other side of the park.

My preliminary assessment shows a number of minor abrasions, a broken left clavicle and a likely broken left ankle. Bleeding is not a problem. Transportation is. The only vehicle in sight is the motorcycle, which the driver has started. I sling and swath the collarbone with my Kling and a borrowed t-shirt and bad Spanish. I stabilize the ankle as best I can with a wrap. Conversations in the crowd indicate that they, too, would like things finished before the army arrives.

The boyfriend whispers in my ear. "For God, Señor, no police. Please, for God, no police." Considering the whimsy of martial law, the boyfriend voices my sentiments exactly.

"I can ride the motorcycle," the girl says. "The hospital is close. Truly, I can ride."

I don't know the words in Spanish, so I ask in English, "You won't faint?"

A woman's voice in the crowd translates immediately for me. The girl shakes her head. She has good color and has calmed down. I believe her.

An old Maya man with a wide red sash steps forward and says something to the boyfriend in an Indian dialect. He unwinds his sash, and the boyfriend mounts the bike. The girl nods toward the bike and glances across the park at the patrol. They cannot see through the thousands of people what exactly is happening, and are not hurrying. One of the firefighters and I make a chair out of our arms and set her on the bike behind the boyfriend. I snug her tight against his back and the Maya binds them together with his sash. The crowd is quiet. The only sounds now are our heavy breaths and the muffled pop-pop of the little engine.

"It is well," the girl says. "We can go."

"Slow," I say.

He thanks us and putts away through the crowd, gliding toward the hospital like a feather on a lake. The crowd breaks into smiles and a lot of talk in a lot of languages. The soldiers don't bother to ask details when they reach us and no one offers explanations. They seem pleased that whatever it was is over, and the people go back to the raising of the cross.

The cross goes up in a great cheer, unsteady on its guy wires, and I am suddenly surrounded by the most incredible stench that I have ever encountered. It's as though somebody dragged a dead horse up behind me—an extremely dead horse. There is a tug at my shirt and I turn to find an Indian woman, middle age, in a plain, aqua pullover dress. She calls me "Doctor" and points to her foot. It is a monster of flies and black flesh. I swallow hard, swallow again and explain that I'm not a doctor while I secretly pray for some wind. Her foot is so swollen that the skin has split between her toes all the way to her ankle. Her toes are small black dots at the end of a fat purple club. The swelling and discoloration reach to her knee. She says it was a scratch two weeks ago and she walked from Petén, almost three hundred miles, to the city. She is with her teenage son, and they have not been able to find anyone in the city who would treat her. Like most of the catechistas, they have no money. There is no pain anymore, she says. They are sleeping in the street. The country is virtually shut down for the Pope's visit. All the passersby give us a wide berth.

I clean her foot in the fountain and wrap it with the rest of my gauze. I keep a pocketful of antibiotics as my personal anti-dysentery kit, so I give them to her. It is now the hottest part of the day and the park seems filled with a dizzying shimmer of gangrene stink, jostling bodies, rifles, ice cream and posters of the Pope. This woman does not read or write, but her son does, so I write down a list of antibiotics to ask for when he can find a pharmacy open. Prescriptions aren't necessary here, but she is beyond the need of mere medication. If there isn't an amputation soon, there will be a death instead. If the hospital won't admit her through the front door, there may be other ways.

"Find an ambulance at the Pope's mass tomorrow," I tell her. "They will all be there. Get one to take you to the hospital, emergency door. You will lose the foot. At least the foot."

She nods, her eyes dull and listless, a sharp contrast to the glittering excitement in the eyes of the faithful around us.

"If you do not do this," I tell her, "you will die."

"I know," she says.

I am not a rich northamerican, but I empty my pockets for her.

"For food and the pharmacy," I say.

She hugs me, then hobbles away through a sea of Christians who turn from her one by one to hold their noses and curse the stink in muttered Spanish.

The cross is secured with a final cheer, the army detachment smiles their relief, and a light breeze through the blossoms in the park refreshes the air for the afternoon's scheduled appearance of the Christian President-General and for tomorrow's visiting representative of institutional charity, the Pope.

Daughters of Salvador

KIDNAPPING wouldn't enter your mind on an average day in Mexico City. What would enter your mind first thing in the morning would be the calls from the street six flights down: "Milk! Juices of orange, juices of grapefruit, apples! Milk!" In this upstairs apartment, no one has slept since Wednesday. It is Saturday morning, and we are making coffee.

Last Wednesday, eleven men with automatics took Yolanda's two teenage daughters from their grandparents' home in San Salvador. Yesterday Yolanda got the first reliable word here in Mexico City on what happened. It was not a kidnapping, as they had been told by El Salvador's Hacienda Police—it *was* the Hacienda Police. No one group in El Salvador commands more fear. Yolanda, a quiet mother of three in her late thirties, cried all night at the news. Her daughters, Elena and Juanita, are only seventeen and fifteen. Now stories of the Hacienda Police string together the long hours between the day and night.

"Another friend was married with a Danish woman," Yolanda tells me. "She spoke no Spanish. I taught her. His parents were of my class, very comfortable. One night, my friend and his wife were disappeared and they found them two weeks later in a shallow grave. She was blonde, very beautiful. They did everything to her, everything. They cut off her breasts, pulled the skin from her face. They pulled out his teeth, his fingernails and his eyes. It was a mistake—they had done nothing, they knew nothing."

The spoon that clinks across the cream-and-sugar silence beats back the unspoken, the unasked.

My back is to a wide bank of windows. Sunlight stutters and catches, melts off the still chill of the high mountain air. Yolanda's geraniums bunch beside me against the glass, their blooms nodding dull scarlet under the smoke and the neglect. Ferns lean towards the windows, too, and an old umbrella-tree watches from the corner. Yolanda calles her plants "daughters."

"I had so many plants in El Salvador that they filled the house," she says. "When we came here we had nothing. We had our clothes that we wore, everything else we left behind. For awhile I felt bad that we had to leave our country, that the girls had to go to new schools, new friends. It is difficult to find work here, when so many Mexican people have no jobs. I was becoming more depressed, so my friends started bringing me plants. Now every morning for five minutes I talk to them. Except this week. . . ."

Back in the girls' bedroom, on their nightstands, lie pictures of their boyfriends, their school friends from Mexico and El Salvador. Juanita's book for Sagittarians brought her no warnings from the stars. There is no television in this house, but Elena's shelf holds well-thumbed copies of *Huckleberry Finn*, *The Sun Also Rises*, *The Mentor Book of Major American Poets*, and Neruda's *Twenty Love Poems*. Three cloth dolls lean together at the top of her orange-crate shelf: one black, one brown and one blonde.

Today, finally, there is better news: Juanita has been released by the Hacienda Police into the custody of her grandparents, Yolanda's very conservative mother and father. The grandparents refuse to let Juanita leave the country or contact her mother. They send a curt message to Yolanda: "Stop calling Salvador. It can only make things worse. The girls should stay here."

Yolanda's parents, extreme rightists, accuse her of working for the FMLN, El Salvador's leftist revolutionary coalition. Yolanda's uncle is the commander of the Hacienda Police. It was her own uncle who had the girls taken to a clandestine jail for interrogation.

"I spoke on the radio for Monsignor Romero," she explains. "I announced the news and was not political, there was none of the rhetoric that others use. That was because it was *Monsignor's* radio station, and because it was his, my parents think I am a communist. That is the way of it in El Salvador. If you are not with the right and not with the left, then they put you with the left anyway and it becomes the same thing for you. After Monsignor was shot I did his eulogy and that was the end for me. But not for them. They sent a death squad after me twice. The first time our northamerican friend here and I outran them. . . ."

"We got lost," Carolyn says, "but they got more lost."

"Yes," Yolanda laughs, "I was just learning to drive. We had servants for that. I am still always lost in a car. We were very lucky, you and I. After you left, we were not so lucky. They came to my Aunt's house by mistake. She has the same name—that was how I found out. The night I found out we had to leave, it was raining, raining hard and my ex-husband called to tell me, 'Don't go out. I will send the girls to you, they have a message.' So I am worried because the tires on the car are not good and the road is very bad with barricades. Elena does not have a license or papers for the roadblocks. It becomes ten-thirty (after curfew), and I start to cry. Ten forty-five, and I am praying for the girls.

"At five to eleven, they touch the door and they are soaked. Elena parked the car blocks away so they would not be followed. The girls tell me the Hacienda Police have made the mistake (of bombing the wrong house.) They do not know about this apartment, they think I am still with my husband. The girls say I have two things to do: live clandestine inside El Salvador or leave the country. We have to decide now. 'Please, Mommy, leave the country,' Elena begged me. 'We can't be with you if you hide here. And every morning on the way to school we'll wonder if one of the bodies in the street is yours.'

"So we decide to leave. I cannot go from the house, so Elena does it all. You know, on the way to school early in the mornings are the bodies—they haven't been moved yet, and so sometimes Juanita would say, 'Oh, Mommy, look—that one doesn't have hands. . . .'

"The police were in front of my parents' house, so Elena could only bring out a few things for me. She brought my one most elegant dress. My sister gave me her rings, bracelets and necklaces and said, 'Here, you can sell these when you get to Mexico.' The Jesuits got up a collection and gave us three hundred dollars. That was all we had when I got to Mexico. It took four days to get out of the country."

There continues to be no news from Elena, only word from Juanita that Elena has been tortured, that she signed what she thought was a record of her belongings, and it became a confession of complicity with the FMLN. After almost two hours of silence, Yolanda picks up the story of her flight out of El Salvador.

"We went through the Spanish ambassador, though I didn't stay in the embassy because it was too difficult to get out. Some people have been forced to stay in embassies for months, longer. So he told me, 'When the time comes, I will have an official car for you and an escort. You will be safe in the car, but once you get out of the car in the airport we can no longer keep them from picking you up.' So it took four days, and on the fourth day everything was ready.

"My ex-husband made a reservation for me with just my initials. I wore my elegant dress and all the jewelry, then hid in the back seat of the car while the girls drove me to the embassy. There I got a surprise. The man who was supposed to accompany me was a man I'd known socially. We'd been to cocktail parties, he played chess with my husband. He said, '*You're* the one . . . !' and I thought he was going to refuse. He started to sweat immediately and it poured from him for the rest of the time we were together.

"He drove me to the airport and did a very brave thing. Instead of letting me out, he got out, too, put his arm around me and pretended that we were lovers saying good-bye. Every time a police patrol came around, he would tuck me up against him and turn my face away. They were not expecting someone so well-dressed. But the plane didn't leave on time. Not for one hour, two hours, three hours. There was a lot of sweat in three hours. It is a small airport.

"Finally, we could leave and he asked permission to walk me onto the plane to say good-bye. He was a very brave, very frightened man. When the plane took off, I cried and couldn't stop. The stewardesses thought I was crying for my lover, but I was crying for my poor country, for my family."

A friend comes with all the day's papers and we go through them for news of the girls and for possible people to contact who might have some influence among El Salvador's rightists. In the San Salvador daily paper we find a group of northamericans who are scheduled to meet with President Magaña on Monday. We catch them at their hotel in San Salvador. Though there is no official news of the girls, at least the Faculty Committee on Human Rights in El Salvador has their names, family details and probable location. They promise to push the President to see them on Monday. Wherever we turn, everyone reaffirms that there can be no news of the girls before Monday.

More coffee.

Yolanda takes up the smoking that she quit after leaving El Salvador, my northamerican partner takes up the smoking that *she* quit after leaving El Salvador and I can see that I am liable to take it up for the first time. Yolanda sips coffee at the dining table, smokes slowly and tells of another Salvadoran friend living in Mexico City.

"He was told he was in danger," she says, rubbing her eyes, "that the Hacienda Police would pick him up. He taught at the University. Before he could go away—he had a wife and two small kids to get out—he was picked up. But his family was powerful, too, and in two weeks he got out. He came to Mexico City to start a new life and was going to send for his family. Three weeks later his wife was picked up leaving the office at the University. They did everything to her, too, then they skinned her until she died. Now his two children are with him here in Mexico, but they never speak, never look up at you when you talk to them.

"This is my country, my family. *These* are the people who took my daughters. My daughter, she can tell them nothing. She knows nothing. But they won't believe that. They'll just keep after her. She's only seventeen, and a very beautiful girl."

Another cigarette in silence, a change of subject.

"I work hard in my job. I make $185 a month, it is a good job." Yolanda prepares advertising copy for newspaper and radio. "It is a kind of writing."

She tells stories of Salvadoran upper class, her people, of how a married woman who begins to study at the University is not praised or helped by her family but suffers the additional frustrations inflicted by fear, suspicion and scorn.

"It bothers them that they can't imagine why I go to school, why I want to do something on my own. Women of my class do not work," she emphasizes her words with the baton of her cigarette. "They go to cocktail parties and look beautiful, though even that won't get you conversation with the northamerican wives. You are to care for your children, your house. You have servants for both. The man gives you everything and you care for it. I had to learn everything—how to drive, to look for a place to live, to look for work in a country that has no work for its own people. I have been very lucky, very lucky. Monsignor looks out for me."

For Yolanda, Monsignor Romero is already a saint.

A woman on the roof across the street folds clothes in a cage. The chicken-wire mesh keeps the birds off the clothes while they dry. She folds them onto a canvas hammock hung from the frame of the cage.

"There will be no news until Monday," a Salvadoran friend says. "Tomorrow let's get out of here and show the northamericans the city."

The northamericans don't argue. Yolanda has spent these past four days moving in the slow, stunned manner of a driver who walks around the wreckage that was her car. The apartment is awash with people and calls, and none of the calls is the right one. All of us, northamerican or not, are ready to get out and see the city. Any of it.

Early Sunday afternoon, downtown, traffic and weather are both clear. As the Avenue of the Lost Child approaches the center of Mexico City it becomes the Avenue St. John, then intersects with the Avenue of the Republic of El Salvador. We take the Republic of El Salvador to the Twentieth of November and it opens up into the central square of the Republic of Mexico.

The Zocaló, the city center, has been the seat of government and religion in Mexico since 1325, when the Aztecs built their capital, Tenochtitlán, on an island in the center of a large, marshy lake. The temple of the Aztecs now lies under four million cars and fifteen million pairs of feet. Only a small section of the temple is under excavation and recovery. The Aztec presence is strong in Mexico City. Serpents and masks, spiritual creatures and geometrics join the statues of saints that busy the front of the Metropolitan Cathedral.

Outside, the beggars claim their stoops and women cook tortillas and cakes over charcoal. In a nook between the cathedral and the Aztec temple a child squats to relieve himself, his hands covering his averted face.

"For Mexico, tomorrow may be what Salvador has today," Yolanda says. "The economy is so bad here, and it is happening so fast." Still, in Mexico City there are not the squads in the streets with assault rifles. No barricades. "I am very much afraid for this country," she says. "I pray for this country."

We drive to the park they call the Mariachi's Park. It is filled with musicians who cluster around benches, power poles, and at the intersections of the paths. Though all of the bands dress in black, each member embroiders himself into distinction. The few women hold babies or beg, none holds an instrument. Marimbas and guitars are the guts of these bands. The lungs are concertinas and trumpets. Solo musicians, duos of musicians, trios and throngs all scatter the park's one-block perimeter. It is winter, most of the trees in the park are bare and no one stands still for long. In Mexico City today, the chill air is frantic with the clashes of musics.

Across the street, a harmonica player in a postal uniform celebrates the entrance to the lunch market, which stays open all night. It reminds me of a building at the Western Washington Fair back home—a long barn, open on three sides, converted to rows of one-booth food stands. Here there are ribs of pork and lamb, broiled strips of beef, ice cream and puddings. Seafood stands back up a bakery and a dessert bar. The harmonica player follows us and wrings a strangled tune into the ear of our Salvadoran friend. It is worth three pesos to save the tune. Lamb ribs hissing from the grill are perfect.

"Both of the northamericans went to Catholic school, too," the friend tells Yolanda. "It is Sunday. We should take them to the convent." They wink at our hesitation.

"Don't worry," Yolanda whispers. "It's a bar."

The convent is a restaurant; it is the old chapel that is now the bar. Over white wine and cheeses and the birds settling down for the night in the garden we talk about love, and about men and women; the history of men and women, the history of nations.

"When people settled your country, they were the best people, good minds, and they intended to live there for all their lives. When people came here it was soldiers, men who came to take back as much wealth as they could. To be stationed in the new world for a long time was not a reward.

"They killed the men, raped the women, destroyed the buildings and carried back what they could to retire in Spain or elsewhere. That is still the pattern in Salvador today. That is a big difference between us."

When we leave we tip the man in khaki for watching the car. He guides us out of the parking place and snaps a salute as we pull away. Back at the apartment there is no place to park. The theater around the corner is showing a movie and people are lined up for an hour and a half before showtime.

"What's the movie that's so popular?" I ask.

"'Desaparacido,'" is the answer. "'Missing.'"

All day Monday, nothing. It is the first day that the representative from the Faculty Committee on Human Rights in El Salvador might be able to see Elena. The phone is shared with the couple next door and passed back and forth on its long cord. No sleep, no news thickens the air and sharpens tongues. At about the time of day that Mexicans stop saying "Good afternoon" and start saying "Good evening," Yolanda's cousin, a lawyer, arrives. She has just come from El Salvador. As of this morning at ten, Elena is being held without charges in Carcel de Mujeres. She describes it as a clean, modern prison for women without conventional cells.

"They show it off to important visitors," she says. "Elena will not be hurt now. She will not be killed there; we can be reasonably sure of that. Classes are taught there. If she is kept for a long time, she will have her schooling."

Yolanda and her cousin hold each other and cry, one relieved of her message and the other relieved of the worst of the very bad fears.

Yolanda laughs through her tears, "I never thought that I would be happy that my girl is in prison."

There is a brandy and its brief comforting warmth. The daily paper that Yolanda's cousin carries from San Salvador accuses a United States congressional delegation due there next week of being ". . . communists and agents of Moscow." The delegation includes Members of Congress, split evenly Republican and Democrat. Among them: Dodd, Ritter, John Glenn. The delegation is scheduled to meet in Mexico City overnight before going on to Guatemala and then El Salvador.

It is then that a light goes on for me, a very chilling light. The day the girls were kidnapped I had just returned from a trip to Guatemala, where I had been training "Rescates," Emergency Medical Technicians, with their fire department. A former Guatemalan army officer had taken me into the highlands to show me a village massacre perpetrated by the army and blamed on the guerrillas. He knew the truth, he had been the officer in charge. He was remorseful, wanted the true story told.

When we got back to Guatemala City, a coup attempt broke out and, since I was traveling with my 14-year-old daughter, I wanted her out of the country. My friend arranged this, but as he drove us to the airstrip he said, "The army has a plan in the works to get your country to free up the helicopter money. They are going to assassinate a prominent American and blame it on the guerrillas."

"Who?"

"I don't know," he said. "I just heard the plan. In the next couple of weeks. They have already disappeared two of your embassy workers, and that wasn't enough. It will be somebody bigger than that."

We said our goodbyes, I promised to come back, and the next day found myself at Yolanda's apartment in Mexico at the bidding of my friend, Carolyn Forché, who worked for Amnesty International. Now, as I read this Salvadoran paper, I know who the prominent American sacrifice would be—John Glenn.

Carolyn, stubborn and articulate, gets us the promise of a few minutes to meet with the delegation at their hotel, but not today. We have permission to bring Yolanda along.

For now, the talk tumbles from everyone at once. The room is full again with neighbors and friends, the scattered nervous laughter of hope, of speculation.

At one time or another it is said in French and English as well as Spanish, and at one time or another it is said by everyone there: "This is a good sign. Maybe they'll let the girls go before anyone has to go in there."

The cousin, the lawyer from Salvador, doesn't really say it herself but she nods in curt encouragement when the notion is presented. After the other visitors leave, Yolanda turns to her cousin and asks, "Isn't it true that there are women in Carcel de Mujeres for two years, three years without charges?"

Once again, but without encouragement, the curt nod.

We take turns throughout the night flurrying and answering calls the length and breadth of the Americas. Tuesday morning, Yolanda goes to work, to her $46 per week. The rest of us make the rounds of pertinent embassies, consulates, hunches and possibilities.

I walk out of the last appointment and onto the first bus that stops. It is the time of the afternoon meal and shopping, buses are athrob with bodies. For three hours, these bodies bear me along from bus to bus, criss-crossing the city. They feel good, these unflinching skins. For a dozen blocks, a matronly woman in black skirt and jacket holds my hand that holds the aisle post and she discusses with the heavily-made-up typist behind her the five acceptable cafés where they could take lunch. Even my poor Spanish knows that this choice comes up between them every day and that each week they try to visit all five cafés but they change the sequence so that they won't get into a rut. Today, they are going to split the lunch special at Vip's, two desserts. At the street where they get out, I catch the next bus home. Everyone who touches me now feels familiar.

Everyone at Yolanda's is napping—on the couch, in chairs—their fatigue gone long beyond denial. Elena's boyfriend yells from the street below for the key. His call is loud, he is obviously excited. He can't stand still, waiting for the drop of the key, and he dances in and out of the cars parked for the movie. He catches the key on the run and covers the six flights up in seconds.

"A-woman-called-me-with-a-message-from-Elena," rattles out in a gasp. "She talked with her yesterday in Carcel de Mujeres and now she's in a hotel downtown and she wants to meet Yolanda."

With one arm in her coat, Yolanda outruns him to the car.

Karen Parker is a blonde northamerican from Berkeley, California, with the Faculty Committee on Human Rights in El Salvador. She speaks flawless Spanish and refuses to be intimidated by bureaucracy in any language. She got our message on Saturday and demanded that President Magaña let her see Elena early Monday morning. After stalling long enough to get Elena presentable, government officials allowed Ms. Parker a few minutes with Elena. The story of what happened to Elena in the custody of the Hacienda Police strips away the evening's sudden joy.

Everyone agrees it could have been worse. That is always a bad concession to make. It does nothing to return Elena. It does not peel the twists of anguish from Yolanda's face.

"She is nervous, now, you understand," Ms. Parker explains. "She has lost weight, but she will receive food in Carcel de Mujeres and the women there look after her. The police will not hurt her any more. Now at least you know it will not get worse for her."

Yolanda walks with Karen alone, comes back walking stiffly, eyes red and eyelids swollen. Beside the wide windows of her apartment, among her plants, she tells us the brief story of Elena's long week.

"You know they took them at two-thirty on the morning that they were to come here. Eleven of them with rifles, civilian clothes, unmarked cars. When my parents said it was a kidnapping, I knew who it was but they wouldn't hear it. The girls' luggage was packed; they took that. Their papers, their passports—those, too. The men took them into my grandparents' bedroom and said, 'Say good-bye to your grandparents.'"

Yolanda has taken a tranquilizer, but her hands still shake enough that her match has difficulty meeting her cigarette.

"Elena thinks that Juanita was not tortured. No one knows for sure, and Juanita will not speak. All we know is that Juanita was kept at the same place in solitary for three days, then released. Elena spent the first thirty-two hours stripped naked, hands tied behind her back, standing. If she moved at all, shifted her position, she was beaten with fists and truncheons. No food, no toilet. Just *them*.

"The whole time a hood was tied over her head, and at irregular intervals she was choked unconscious with a garrotte. Halfway through the second day the beatings stopped. I think all our pressure was getting through to them. They kept her awake for the rest of the week, under the hood, interrogating her for names, for facts she couldn't know. No sleep. The human rights people don't think she ate. It was because someone was there in person to demand to see her, someone who had her name, that they moved her to Carcel de Mujeres. They really wanted me and my ex-husband. They knew that we would come to get the girls out. It was right of you and Carolyn to keep us from going. Then they would have had four people to torture."

She goes on to tell Elena's story of people in the clandestine jail who are no longer recognizable as human beings. How, by day or night, there is no end to the screams, the shrieks and the begging for mercy or death.

This is the night everyone cries. Some of the tears are relief, many of frustation and hatred. Had we the Hacienda Police at our disposal, we might easily become what they are for the moment. The convenience of time and distance keeps us human.

On Thursday, a team of doctors and scientists that is touring El Salvador gets to see Elena and care for her injuries. We finally meet with the congressional delegation that is off to Guatemala and then El Salvador. The Carcel de Mujeres is on their itinerary. At first, the congressmen are much more concerned with whether Yolanda is a communist, as the Salvadoran military claims, than with the welfare of the girls.

"Are you a communist?" John Glenn asks.

"Sir," she replies, "I am a Christian."

I tell them my story, then, to warn them off from Guatemala and try to get them indebted enough to us to trade favors. An aide places a call to Guatemala while I pull out the article from El Salvador that calls them all ". . . communists and agents of Moscow." They are not amused.

The aide comes back, speaks privately to Mr. Glenn, and we settle down to some serious talk. They have cancelled their Guatemala trip, the embassy there received a warning, too, but notified no one about it.

In El Salvador, Glenn and Ritter press hard and Elena is released from the prison. Three weeks later, the family relents and both girls are allowed to come to Mexico to their mother.

So, I am home now, too, in Washington state, watching the tide lick the bank below my window. At odd intervals, between typing these notes I sip coffee, stare out the window and wonder how long my country will have this luxury of distance and time.

Elena was released, and the next day President Reagan confirmed that El Salvador did indeed conform to our notion of human rights. He released forty-two million dollars of military aid, only two months after he'd told reporters that he was going to do it, anyway. The political battle of Elena and Juanita is over, but their emotional battle is just begun.

Still, in El Salvador, the suspension of rights, the policy of snatch, take, grab and keep knows no bounds, not even family.

What Elena Said

"For three days I had no food, no water, nothing," she says. "They beat me and beat me but I didn't really feel it, you know? The adrenalin, I think."

She drags at her cigarette with a *snap* and taps the ashes out the window. It is a sunny afternoon, a dusty back road heading north, and the holiday in this country is the Day of the Dead.

"Like they say about getting shot," she says, "that it doesn't hurt because of the shock. But later, when they took off the blindfold, I hurt so bad I couldn't move. When I saw what they did to me, I hurt."

Elena was a high school senior last year when she stood blindfolded and naked with her thumbs tied behind her back in San Salvador. Today there are six of us in this Volkswagen heading north, now safe and a little drunk in Mexico. The others comment in Spanish on the aroma of the roast chickens we have in the trunk and our low beer supply.

"One day, I don't know which, they left me alone." She laughs a short laugh. "Except I knew I wasn't alone. I had this feeling. And somehow I knew he was drawing. So I asked him, 'What are you drawing?' and he jumped."

Another sudden laugh, another *snap* at her cigarette and the tilt of the ash outside. She smiles.

"He must have been a little frightened," she says.

"'You're watching me!' he said, and I said, 'No, I'm not watching you.' He came over and stuffed tissue inside my blindfold, then he sat down. I could tell after awhile he was throwing a drawing away, so I asked him, 'Why do you throw it away when you work so hard on it?'

"'Stop watching me!'

"You know, Salvadorans are *so* superstitious, so religious that sometimes they are afraid of things like this. I told him again, 'I'm not watching you.'

"'Then how do you know what I'm doing all the time?'

"'I don't know,' I said. 'I just *know.*'

"'Well, stop it,' he said, and came to tighten the blindfold.

"'That hurts my nose,' I told him, 'and my thumbs hurt.'

"That's all I could remember that hurt then, my thumbs where they had them tied tight with the cord. So he said, 'You won't watch me anymore?' And I said, 'I'm not watching you.'

"He loosened the blindfold and the cord around my thumbs. After they took me from my grandparent's place I really wanted a cigarette, but I didn't ask because they trade everything. Everything. They wanted the name of my Mexican boyfriend but I didn't even tell them that because that would be a start. If I started . . . Well, I told this man I would like a cigarette, and he said, 'You will stop watching me?'

"Of course, I told him, 'I'm not watching you.' I couldn't give in, you see, to anything."

A final *snap* at the cigarette and she flips it out the window. It spins in the highway behind us and she lights another.

"So he gave me two cigarettes," she says, "and then the others came back and he left. For three more days no water, no food, no bathroom. I just stood there naked inside that blindfold while they beat me. But I got two cigarettes, and they got nothing."

Solstice and the Soothsayer's Temple
(from *ViraVax*)

COLONEL Toledo received his divorce papers by courier at his new apartment in La Libertad, Costa Brava's capitol city. The fresh paint wasn't dry yet and the stitches in the scissors wound to his neck had just come out this morning. Grace Toledo, slow to anger but quick with the scissors, had taken their son and never looked back. The Colonel had been too drunk to remember what the argument had been about, but he suspected it had been about Rachel.

Toledo crumpled the offensive paperwork, smashed it, tossed it out the open window and into the rest of the garbage strewn in the street. He made a quick call to Rachel at the embassy, tossed back two quick sugared rums, and couldn't stop pacing.

Rachel picked him up a few minutes later in her black Flicker. Rico was in no mood for small talk, so she settled him into the passenger seat with a bottle of Wild Turkey. She waited until they got to her house before she handed him the pouch with the official DIA seal.

"Two in one day," he said. "How lucky can I get?"

Inside he found his severance paycheck and his official suspension on Defense Intelligence Agency letterhead. That, in itself, was a clear message that he was through. Solaris's meticulous left-handed signature smudged in the middle of the "o."

After the Wild Turkey came more sugared rum. With the rum came remorse, rage and a wild ride to the airport.

Rico Toledo woke up tangled in Rachel's arms and legs, their tropical sweat prickling at him where they pulled apart. A muggy heat smothered everything but the familiar aroma of their sex. White sheets exaggerated the contrast in their skins—his, dark and brush-scratched;

hers, schoolgirl pale. He sat up against the headboard, another hang-over hammering his temples.

The Yucatán dawn made a white glow of his pants where he'd slung them across a chair at the bedside. Rico had stitched a ring into the righthand pocket of those pants for safekeeping. Such a treasure should not be flashed among men of the children of the large, wormy bellies. He liked the feel of promise it gave him when he slipped on his pants. Its cool gold never warmed up.

Everything at home had been seized by Grace's lawyers. The Agency's severance pay left him enough to scrape by on for six months, if he stayed in Mexico.

A year, in the States.

But then he would be in the States and that was no picnic, right now. He had set out to prove something by flying to the heart of the Yucatán. After at least two days of nonstop drinking, it was time he found out what.

Rachel Lear was half his age, with red hair and freckles the Latins called "pecas." Unlike the embassy crowd, the campesinos understood that it was not an unnatural thing for a man to love a younger woman. Many of them had been cut by their women, as Grace had cut him, and all of them drank when the bottle passed around. Colonel Toledo, the gringo chameleon, had held a role so long that he had suspended himself like an insect in amber.

Rico marvelled over his turn of luck as he sat naked in the lounge chair. He watched Rachel sprawl face down to fill his hollow in the bed. Her right hand tucked under her cheek, her right leg cocked to her waist. A tuft of red hair reached between her legs for the sky.

The Yucatán was truly a place of magic, a place of ripples in the drapery of time. This was Latin America, but not a war zone. Not even a war country. Rico had fled here twice before. In 1998, he was forgetting a war. In 2010, he brought his ten-year-old and his wife to see the heart of the Mayan empire, and to avoid some ugly but necessary steps that the Agency was taking all over Costa Brava in his absence.

The Colonel's son, Harry, developed histoplasmosis from exploring a Mayan cave, and he nearly died. Rico had spent most of that vacation in a hospital but, like it or not, it made an excellent alibi when he returned to face the new Costa Brava, and the political fallout.

Now Rico came to get a new start. He tried to forget Grace, and that wasn't working. He and Rachel had argued all night. It started . . . well, he pushed it out of mind. That would not discourage him, now, from enjoying the dawn of the day that everything would change.

The white sunlight seared anything that was not stone, adding counterpoint to his headache. Rico pulled on his rumpled clothes and turned the window fan on high. The bearings howled and the blades shrieked against the frame. Not much of a breeze kicked up, and Rachel didn't stir.

Rachel spoke Spanish, but she was shy because she'd learned it in school and most of the embassy staff enveloped themselves in English. She refused to speak except between them, so Rico did most of the talking. She attracted people, men and women, so Rico talked a lot, but talking came pretty natural to Rico, in either language.

It's sure a plus when you're outspooking spooks, he thought.

Rico Toledo, Ex-Colonel, US Army/Defense Intelligence Agency, made a helluva tour guide.

Didn't talk much at home.

Bob or Bonnie, friends of Rachel's from the states, flushed the toilet across the hall. They spoke only English and had paid dearly to get their visas and out of the states. Consular flunkies and federal reps checked their registry at the guest house daily. The United States was not an easy place to leave, these days.

Rico gulped down the warm, flat beer he'd been saving, then poured himself a dark rum. He added sugar and lemon, then carried it to the veranda to sip with the parrot, who asked him his name over and over and over. By the time Rico finished his drink he was restless again and needed to move.

"Get up," he said to Rachel. "Your friends are up and the car's here."

"Don't order me around."

She spoke into her pillow and he could barely understand her.

"Try this, okay? Okay?" she said. "Just tell me that the car's here."

He didn't answer.

"Try it."

Rico poured himself another Flor de Caña, mixed in the sugar and the lemon.

"Okay, okay," she said.

She sat up crosslegged on the bed, her red blaze of pubic hair a challenge for his attention. His attention began to knock at his zipper door.

"If you'd said, 'Rachel, the car's here and your friends are up,' I could've—"

"Can it," Rico said.

He tossed back his sweet, dark rum and left for a coffee with their driver.

Rico and Rachel argued the morning away, mostly in Spanish. They affected a conversational tone, so her stateside friends wouldn't catch on. Of course, their driver knew everything and became more nervous by the kilometer.

Their driver, Carlos, didn't speak English. His left arm had been withered by polio and his car overheated crossing the tiny range of sierras between Mérida and Uxmal. He topped off the radiator with water from a wine bottle. Carlos was a smooth, cautious driver. When the argument with Rachel got more personal than Carlos could bear, he interrupted with a passionate assessment of the American football playoffs. At one point, with all but Carlos and Rico sleeping, a huge buzzard rose from the shoulder of the road and gyred once around the car, its black eye fixed on Rico the whole time. Rachel slept tucked up against him. Her long red hair whipped their faces in the wind.

Carlos launched into the old tale about the Soothsayer's Temple and the sacrificial Ballcourt.

"The man was birthed from a feathered serpent's egg," he said, "and became a man in one night. In one night he built the Pyramid of the Magician, Temple of the Sorcerer. You will see, it is a night's work."

Rico didn't tell Carlos that he'd been here twice before, that he had lived with the Maya years ago and ghosted most of the jungles of the region. Instead, Rico kept him talking.

"And the sacrifice of the Ballcourt?" Rico asked.

Rico could see Carlos was let down by this question, like he'd expected something more from Rico. Even the casual tourist has heard of the sacrificial ballgame of the Mayas. Rico was flattered that Carlos expected better of him.

Carlos shrugged.

"Two teams, with captains. They wear equipment like your football, lots of pads. They try to slap a hard rubber ball through a stone hoop sideways on the wall. The winning team gets to run through the gallery, collecting jewelry and favors from the nobles. If the weather has been bad for crops, the winning captain has the honor of being killed. To save his people."

Carlos didn't seem interested in elaborating and recited this lecture in a bored monotone.

"How did they do it?"

A sigh, a *thump* of the withered limb against the car door.

"Cut throat, cut off head, open chest and take out heart," Carlos said.

He added the appropriate gestures.

"Efficient," Rico admitted.

Carlos shrugged.

"The ballcourt is nothing," he said. "The Magician's Temple, that is very special." Carlos repeated, with a nod, "Very special."

"What makes it special?"

"The place, the earth that it is on. Its position in that place. The centuries. You will see." Carlos nodded his head at Rachel. "It will be good for you, the Temple. You will see."

Then he stopped the station wagon on the shoulder to add his last jug of water to the radiator. The only mountain pass that Carlos had ever driven was this one saddle across the only crest on the limestone plateau. It was a hundred meters high at the summit. The only other breaks in the terrain for two hundred klicks were temples.

Carlos explained how sunset and moonrise faced off on the diagonal at the top of the Wizard's Temple, making the inner chambers into alternating geometrics of silver and gold, shadow and light. The staircase casts an undulating serpent of shadow against the walls once a year, and tonight was the night.

". . . and you stand inside, at the top, and let the shadows divide you. Then good and bad will leave your body: good to the light and bad to the shadow. You walk out with your luck for the rest of your life."

His glance shifted from the road to Rico's eyes, back again. Then back.

"Who told you this?" Rico asked. "A teacher?"

"No, no teacher. Uncle. He was a bad one, my friend, and he came back cured of the women and mezcal."

"Do you think I can be cured?"

This was the first time Rico spoke of the argument, of his relationship with the young woman. It felt possible in Spanish.

Carlos softened his voice almost to a whisper.

"There is no cure for love, friend," he said, but the word he used for "cure" was "salvation." He rattled his bent left arm against his door and shrugged a twisted fist skyward. "If my uncle is right, if there are these devils, then I will walk away from them tonight."

Rico had no idea at the time that "tonight" meant "midnight" and "I" meant "we."

They drove awhile in the relative silence of the road and the countryside.

Rico felt Rachel's breathing shift. Now she stretched, and looked around, and Carlos aimed his attention straight ahead. Rachel's eyes shone with an ice-light: cold, blue and clear. Earlier this morning, driving the scrub jungle mist at dawn, they had been a lush, snakeskin green.

By the time the five of them got to Uxmal, their eyes were tired from too much sun off the hood and everything seemed hazed in light, a fine white wash. Carlos preferred to wait with his car in a patch of shade, so they cleared the guard gate without him and walked to the foot of the Temple of the Magician. A busload of American college students climbed the steep face in a gusting wind, all shouting to one another in rude, idiomatic English.

To the left hunched a lone Jaguar statue, an altar. Several of the young people gathered around this one. Rico explained the Jaguar and fertility to Rachel and their friends, the Agency's briefing version. From somewhere on the breeze came a whiff of tortillas hissing over charcoal.

A fat American girl about Rachel's age jumped onto the statue, clasping its head in her dimpled thighs. Another girl shrieked, then turned to the rest and shouted, "Tim, Brian! Shelley sat on its face! You guys, it was *so* funny! She sat on his *face!*"

"Must've been too big to get her mouth around it," one boy commented, and they all laughed.

Rachel's friend Bob reached for an empty Coke bottle that leaned against the Jaguar's shoulder, but a little dark-eyed boy snatched it up first.

Rico pulled them away in disgust. He and Rachel wandered the stones under a reddening sun and climbed the Wizard's Temple just before sunset. Everyone else came down early, afraid of the treacherous footholds and the rising shadows.

Shadows clarified the open spaces between the sacrificial ballcourt and the scrub jungle skirting the compound. A few stragglers walked the ballcourt below. Every word they spoke rang true to Rico four hundred meters away. Every grunt and cry of the ballplayers must have been heard by all. It was a ceremonial game, a great prayer to cheer on the restoration of happiness and plenty.

Rico toyed with the ring in his right pants pocket. He wondered whether marrying Rachel would be the right thing. It would be respectable, and not at all what anyone would expect.

Especially Grace, he thought.

Another buzzard circled twice, then trailed out of sight somewhere towards Costa Brava. The scrub jungle around the temples reminded him of his first meeting with his dead friend, Red Bartlett. The young Red came down to please his wife and to hone his broken Spanish. Like Rico, he had stayed, seduced by the ultimate opiate of doing what he loved. That was a lifetime ago.

Bartlett's lifetime.

Rachel and the other couple waited on the veranda of the temple, but Rico stood inside, watching them and shooting pictures through the archway.

"What's the matter?" Rachel asked, with a childlike shrug, "can you see through my dress?"

Rico had been staring from the shadows. She stood in the doorway of the temple, her body backlighted by sunset and a glorious rising moon that just fit its shoulders into the frame of the entrance around her. A sharpness in the setting of the ring in his pocket bit at an infected hangnail on his finger.

"Nothing's the matter," he said, "just daydreaming. Yes, I can see through your dress."

They stood inside a stone doorway atop the Sorcerer's Pyramid, a doorway that framed tonight's moonrise over sunset perfectly. This room had been the Magician's personal quarters. Bats chittered from the beam-holes. Outside, crickets and cicadas quieted with the rising of the moon. When it came time to give her the ring, Rico didn't know why he asked her what he did.

"I thought we were going to drop it," she said.

Those soft lips thinned into a hard gray line. Her freckles stood out in the rising moonlight, distinct in a dead sort of way, like bruised scales.

"I can't drop it."

"What do you need to know for, anyway?"

"Because you don't want to tell me."

Rico's heart was slamming along pretty fast, and he had the shakes a little bit. Hunting used to make him feel that way. Slipping around in a war at night made him feel that way.

The shadow of the hooked arm of their driver snaked across the temple wall behind Rico like a great plumed serpent, encircling Rachel's head and shoulders. It was all an illusion of shadow, but in an eyeblink it boosted Rico's heartbeat even more.

"We must go now," Carlos announced. "They are locking up, there will be trouble and a fine."

Rico thanked him. Rachel took Rico's hand and they called the others. When the going got rough Rachel picked her way ahead of him. He got two great shots of her silhouette against the moonlit stones. Her pale dress fanned out like wings in the breeze, the red splash of her hair the only real color left against the gray.

They met Carlos on the path and two muttering guards locked the gates behind them.

"Do you know how you're going to get back in?" Rico asked him.

"Yes," he said. "What about the others?"

"I haven't asked them. Everyone is hungry and thirsty, no? Let's go to the mission that we passed. After dinner I will ask."

"For this, for the rest of the night, you are the guests of me and my car."

Rico thanked him, as though he had a choice, but courtesy demanded it.

"There are snakes," Carlos warned. "Serpientes."

He repeated the word for Rachel's sake, but to her credit she didn't flinch.

"There are cenotes, wells. They drop out from under you in this earth here. It falls in sometimes and swallows you up."

"When was the last time?"

Carlos shrugged.

"I don't know. People just say."

Village women glided in with the unsubtle dusk. Their arms resembled great wings, draped as they were with merchandise. Green- and blue-bordered sashes trailed them like fragile tail feathers. They held the dresses to Rachel and smoothed them out, sweeping her blaze of hair where they wanted it for effect in the dim light, *just so.* Their eyes reflected coffee and candlelight.

Rachel bought a white dress, a pretty one that immediately came unstitched, but it was that warm, happy time of evening just as the mosquitoes come out.

They downed a few beers at the mission bar, then dinner. Carlos stuck to Diet Coke and cigarettes that he snapped out of the pack to his lips in a graceful, one-handed flick. The others liked the idea. Rico knew they would.

Then Bob told them about the duct tape in his bag.

"For around the doors in the hotel in case there's a fire," he said. "But we could make a ball out of it and play on the court. That would be a trip."

Rachel and Bonnie laughed and toasted, "Yeah, let's do it!"

They had two hours to kill. Carlos paced it off outside.

When Rico stepped outside for air, Carlos showed him the path. A power line strung out from the mission in a straight line to the temple grounds, for the tourist shop. Scrub brush came chest-high to Rico and wasn't hard going except for the bugs.

Chiggers in the grass bit them up around the ankles. They were just drunk enough and the moon bright enough that they made it, still a little tipsy, sweating under the ivory disc of a moon. Bob's duct-tape ball was a silver blur against the stones of the ballcourt wall.

"Remember," Bonnie called out from some shadow to Rico's right, "winning captain gets sacrificed."

"Only on special occasions," Rachel said.

She let go Rico's hand and slapped the makeshift ball into the wall. It skidded, sparkling up along the stones in a long, smooth arc.

"You have to be quiet down there," Carlos hissed, "the guards will hear."

Rachel tugged Rico's sleeve.

"Where are you going? Don't you want to play?"

"Yeah," he said. "But I want to see the moon now from the top. Then I'll come down and play."

"You won't," she said. "You always say you will, but you won't."

The ringstone in his pocket irritated his right thigh with every step up the steep stairway of the temple. It seemed to grow heavier, colder.

"Play ball!" Bob said in a clear whisper.

Rico turned to watch Rachel run off to the game. He topped the temple stairs, conscious of the beer numbing his feet, toying with his balance. At the top, Carlos stood over a diagonal line of white stone inlaid across the floor. Rico straddled the line, back to Carlos. Over the guide's malformed shoulder, the swollen moon.

The doorsill at the tips of Rico's feet dropped away down the rough stone face to the ballcourt plaza. Now the moon polished the face of the stonework and lit up the countryside. All around them birdsongs started up, sleepy and confused at the light. The scent of allspice and bougainvilla hung in the humid stillness of the night.

The moon sighted down the diagonal between Rico's feet. He did not feel a particular pull towards either side.

Bob scored below, his duct-tape ball *thwocketed* through the ancient stone goal. They were all excited and a little bit drunk yet, so it wasn't surprising that Rachel called him by the wrong name. It was one that Rico had heard her use by mistake instead of his own.

"*Bob,*" she corrected herself, "I'm sorry. I meant 'Yeah, *Bob*, nice shot!'"

Rico's problem, the thing that started their argument in the first place, had to do with that particular name. Suddenly Rico stood awash in light. The shadow had swept aside while he was distracted and now he heard other voices down below, speaking abrupt and agitated Spanish. Behind him, Carlos sighed and shuffled forward. He patted Rico's back with his good arm.

"We'd better go down," Carlos said. "Now we will all be fined. There is trouble. I hope you and your friends have money."

Carlos flexed his left arm a couple of times before they started down.

"The arm," Rico asked him, "will it work?"

Carlos shrugged in his way, intent on the footing. The moonlight's angle dazzled them on their climb down, the way it reflected so brightly off the stone.

"Perhaps with exercise," Carlos said.

When they were nearly down and the four guards approached with the others, Carlos asked, "And your woman? The girl?"

"It is lost," Rico said. "Perhaps another time."

The guards might have settled for a private sum and the whole matter could have been dropped right there. The chief of the guards delicately insisted that he and his men had standards. Bob indelicately shoved a wad of money under his nose before Rico could intervene.

The next morning in the city, Rico sold his plane ticket and paid off the fine against Carlos and the station wagon.

Carlos drove Rachel and the others to the airport while Rico sold his ring to a thin, unhappy-looking jeweler above the courthouse. It came to quite a pile of pesos. By the time Carlos pulled in with his radiator steaming, Rico had already moved into the spare room, the small one out on the porch with all the light.

Notes

About the Author

BILL RANSOM, acclaimed author of *Burn, ViraVax, The Ascension Factor* (with Frank Herbert), and other novels, also has a long list of credits in poetry, short fiction, and journalism. Over the past twenty-five years, his work has been published by large New York houses, by small presses, in commercial anthologies, in newspapers large and small. His novels have been compared to Crichton's, Clancy's and Follett's; his short stories have been supported by the PEN/NEA Syndicated Fiction Project; and his poetry has been nominated for the Pulitzer Prize.

In *Learning the Ropes*, Ransom collects a sampling of his best work, including short fiction, essays and poems, along with excerpts from two of his novels. Ransom addresses a wide range of experience, from up-close encounters with Central American death squads to the "delicacy the morning has with hairs." As a "creative autobiography," *Learning the Ropes* is both a retrospective on the work of a gifted writer at mid-career, and a fascinating multi-genre statement in its own right.

"I miss you too. . . ." They were standing very close to each other. She'd only have to move her other hand a little to touch his chest. Like this. She looked into his warm eyes, hardly able to believe he was with her. He'd come back.

"Will . . . am I being stupid if I do this?" Anna slid her hand to his shoulder.

He smiled, and her heart lifted. "No."

She swallowed. "Or this?" She touched the back of his neck and tilted her face towards him.

"No," he said, his mouth inches from hers.

"Or this . . ."

"Stop talking and get on with it."

Anna sighed happily. "Okay."

Anna died inwardly. Too painful. Move on. Everyone else managed to move on. She put her hand on the door handle. "Let's go back. This rain doesn't look like it's going to let up and I must change before the meeting."

"Anna—" He caught her hand as it turned the door handle. "Are you running away?"

She shrugged, feeling unable to speak, his hand on hers.

"What are you frightened of?" Will said gently.

"Being stupid," she whispered, unable to look at him. "I've been stupid so much. . . ."

"You're not stupid," he said. "Anything but."

Anna moved her hand from Will's to the glass, feeling it cold against her palm, hardly daring to hope. "What are you frightened of?" she said.

"Hamsters."

"What?" The answer caught her by surprise and she laughed.

"All vets are," Will said with an apologetic shrug, but the twinkle in his eyes she remembered. "They've got a really vicious bite, and the more scared they are, the harder they bite, and worse, you've got some kid watching you with enormous eyes as you're yelling blue murder and trying to flick little Hammy off your hand."

His voice trailed away. The raindrops pelted the windows, blurring the view of the garden into impressionistic sweeps of green and gray. Will looked out at the rain, his face serious. "When I came to Temple-combe I thought I'd never feel anything again. Then you arrived, and . . . That day, when I saw you with Oliver . . . it hurt. The woman I thought you were no longer existed, she was someone I had imagined. Then in the temple—I didn't trust what had happened. I couldn't. It was too per-fect, too incredible. I didn't deserve it." He sighed. "When I left I didn't intend to come back. I had to sort my life out, and you weren't part of it. Or so I thought." He stopped and turned to her. "I know I've got no right coming back here and expecting . . . hoping . . ." His voice was very soft and gentle, so quiet she could hardly hear him. "I miss you."

He misses me. He misses me. Anna stared at the gray rain, but inside she felt like a million fireworks were exploding, filling her soul with flashes of light and energy and joy. *He misses me.*